The Jobs Crisis

edited by
Colm Keane

The Thomas Davis Lecture Series
General Editor: Michael Littleton

Published in association with
Radio Telefís Éireann
by

MERCIER PRESS

Mercier Press Ltd
PO Box 5, 5 French Church Street, Cork *and*
24 Lower Abbey Street, Dublin 1.

ISBN 1 85635 053 3

A CIP catalogue record for this book
is available from the British Library

The Thomas Davis Lectures
General Editor: Michael Littleton
Every autumn, winter and spring since September 1953, Radio
Telefís Éireann has been broadcasting half-hour lectures, named in
honour of Thomas Davis. Inspired by one of his famous sayings,
'Educate that you may be free', the aim of these lectures has been to
provide in popular form what is best in Irish scholarship and the
sciences.

Most of the lectures have been in series form; many have been
single broadcasts; some have been in English; some in Irish. In the
time that has passed since they were initiated, the lectures have
dealt with many aspects and with many centuries of Irish social
life, history, science and literature. The lecturers, distinguished for
their special learning at home and abroad, have been drawn from
many nations but mainly from Ireland.

Printed in Ireland by Colour Books Ltd.

Contents

Acknowledgements

The editor and publishers wish to thank The Saw Doctors and songwriters Mr Leo Moran and Mr Davy Carton for permission to quote from 'Sing a Powerful Song' from the Saw Doctors album, *If this is Rock 'n Roll I Want My Old Job Back*.

List of Contributors

Colm Keane	Senior Producer, RTE Radio
Colm McCarthy	Director, DKM Economic Consultants
Fintan O'Toole	Columnist, *The Irish Times*
Dr Garret FitzGerald	Commentator and Lecturer
Mike Allen	General Secretary, Irish National Organisation of the Unemployed
Raymond Crotty	Research Associate, Department of Statistics, Trinity College, Dublin
Peter Cassells	General Secretary, Irish Congress of Trade Unions
Gearóid Ó Tuathaigh	Associate Professor of History, University College, Galway
J.J. Lee	Professor of Modern History, University College, Cork
Brendan Halligan	Chairperson, Institute of European Affairs
Brendan Walsh	Professor of the National Economics of Ireland, University College, Dublin
David Kennedy	Professor of Strategic Marketing, University College, Dublin

Paddy Walley   Director, Institute for Enterprise
                                and Innovation, Ireland

John Kenneth Galbraith   Paul M. Warburg Professor of
                                Economics Emeritus, Harvard
                                University

Introduction

Colm Keane

ON 8 JANUARY 1978 the then Taoiseach, Jack Lynch, was interviewed on RTE's 'This Week' programme. Jobs and the Government's employment policy were discussed. He was asked, if unemployment rose to 100,000 would the electorate be right to put him out of office? 'Absolutely,' Mr Lynch replied, 'I think they would be well justified if there are that many ... if we don't deliver then the electorate are entitled to put us out of office.' It was an ominously prophetic remark.

Mr Lynch's comment would become a definitive bench-mark in the history of Irish unemployment. The Irish economy would no longer see unemployment levels of 60,000 or 70,000 which were so common in the early 1970s. Instead, by the time Fianna Fáil lost office in June 1981, the Live Register had jumped to over 123,000. By 1982 over 150,000 were unemployed. By 1983 the figure topped 200,000. By 1986 over a quarter of a million were on the dole. And in January 1993, unemployment crashed through the 300,000 barrier, establishing a new bench-mark in Irish unemployment history. Within 15 short years we have come a long way.

The summer of 1992 was a black summer for jobs. August brought a spate of redundancies in Dublin, Limerick, Longford and Tuam. Waterford Crystal, Wang, Coillte Teo all sought job losses. It was also the month that RTE commissioned 'The Jobs Crisis' series. Thirteen lecturers were selected to analyse the crisis. Their remit was to examine what had gone wrong and what could be done, if anything. Their papers were delivered in the Thomas Davis Lecture slot on RTE Radio One. It is these papers that are contained in this book and collectively they amount to a comprehensive study of the crisis that has brought record numbers onto Irish dole queues.

Irish unemployment statistics make for disturbing reading. Current Irish unemployment rates are the highest in the history of the State, the worst in the EC and almost twice the EC average. More than 125,000 people are long-term unemployed and over 90,000 people under 25 are without work. Over one-half of our unemployed are crammed into the urban centres of Dublin, Cork, Galway and Limerick. As Raymond Crotty puts it, 'Fewer people get a livelihood in Ireland now than at any time in the past 250 years, a period during which the world's population and its workforce have increased over sevenfold.' Continuing the theme, Colm McCarthy says, 'There is no country with which Ireland can reasonably be compared which has such a high unemployment rate, and those countries regard their unemployment levels as unacceptable.'

So why have we allowed the crisis to deepen? Why has it all got so out of hand? Mike Allen, who has experienced unemployment, suggests that, 'The Irish people have faced an unemployment problem so severe and so protracted that we have come to see it as a natural phenomenon.' Fintan O'Toole reaches a similar conclusion. 'We have,' he says, 'produced a political culture that is remarkably at home with the idea of mass unemployment and remarkably pessimistic about the prospects of doing anything about it.' Dr Garret FitzGerald points to the public and political ambivalence about the sacrifices needed to tackle unemployment. Outstanding political leadership is required, he says, but given the public's ambivalence, 'it is, I believe, unrealistic to expect from politicians such exceptionally courageous leadership.'

If 'The Jobs Crisis' lectures had one main objective it was not just to analyse the causes of unemployment, but to take a positive look at the issues and to examine the options for employment creation. 'Growth on its own won't create jobs,' says Peter Cassells. 'We need an entrepreneurial revolution in this country. We will have to stop thinking of business people as confined to those who were born with a silver spoon in their mouth or those who went from rags to riches by suspect means.' Paddy Walley takes up the challenge of the future, the new information technology, new opportunities in service employment, research, design, marketing and customer service. 'If we do not open our way of looking at the future,' he says, 'then we will inevitably reproduce the past with all its problems, not least the problem of unemployment.'

 Tax reform, wage cuts, public expenditure controls, social welfare reform, new industrial development strategies, local development initiatives, legislative reform are just some of the remedies that appear in the following papers. Most urgently, there is a call for a clear Government strategy. 'There is no lack of action,' says Joe Lee. 'But it is mindless action, ad hoc action responding in an incoherent manner to perceived short-term problems ... We do not know how to think strategically, however repeatedly we now use the word "strategy". His view is echoed by David Kennedy, who argues that the new national focus must be centred on unemployment. 'A country in a national emergency, such as war,' he says, 'marshals all of its national resources in order to survive and my first suggestion is that such a single-minded focus is needed today.'

Yet fashions change quickly. Established policies are discredited. Discredited policies are rehabilitated and old beliefs are given new meaning. Take the revival of John Maynard Keynes, an economist from the 1930s whose theories might just fit the 1990s. Mrs Thatcher is gone. President Clinton is in office. And a new Irish Government is formed with Labour Party participation. Brendan Walsh assesses the change, perceptible but not yet dramatic. 'Keynesianism,' he says, 'to the extent that it is enjoying a comeback, is limited to advocating that high levels of government spending and taxation are almost inevitable and may even help promote economic growth.' But he continues, 'No Irish economist has urged the new Government ... to embark on tax cuts and increased spending in order to bring the rate of unemployment down.'

John Kenneth Galbraith, the celebrated 'Keynesian' economist from Harvard University, also takes up the issue. 'We must,' he says, 'as an exercise in common everyday caution and good sense, accept in the larger world the proposition that Keynes articulated: the modern economy does not necessarily find its equilibrium at full employment.' So what is the remedy? Professor Galbraith advocates that we accept budget deficits, at least in the short run. 'The economic activity and employment so provided is the only design for dealing with the depressive equilibrium that ... does not depend on fragile theory. It goes directly to the needed result,' he says.

Looking to Europe, there is renewed hope from the Structural Funds, promising a windfall of £8 billion by the end of the century. With proper strategies and proper policies, Brendan Halligan says, these structural funds could develop our food, forestry and fishing industries to the point of self-sustaining growth. But more is required: a new transport strategy to link us to the heart of Europe, a new range of linguistic skills, more research and development, a coherent policy framework formulated by government.

Staying with Europe, Gearóid Ó Tuathaigh examines the regional dimension, arguing that the structural funds are not likely to bring about convergence between the EC regions. He says, 'In the short- to medium-term, some towns and villages will lose more jobs and will be further bled by the haemorrhage of emigration. The loss of population and of key institutions ... may further loosen the social bonds and damage the morale of more rural communities, leaving them lingering on in a sad state of social anæmia.'

THERE ARE many people who gave generously of their time in compiling *The Jobs Crisis*. I am particularly grateful to

Professor John Kenneth Galbraith for his unfailing courtesy and kindness. We are honoured to have him in the series. My thanks are due to Michael Littleton of RTE for his comments and guidance. I would also like to mention Emer Ryan of Mercier Press, Úna O'Hagan and Seán Keane for their patience. Above all, I must thank the contributors for the thought and effort they put into their lectures. Their work deserves to be studied widely and with great care.

1. A Review of the Crisis

Colm McCarthy

DURING THE GENERAL election of November 1992, and through the long-drawn-out process of forming a government which ensued, we have heard a great deal about unemployment in Ireland. The politicians have been unanimous in identifying unemployment as the principal economic policy problem facing the country, and in this they reflect the perceptions of the general public as recorded in several opinion polls.

They have also been forthcoming with proposals for addressing the unemployment problem, to which I will return later. But a characteristic of the political analysis of the present dilemma, and one which I find particularly revealing, is the failure of any party to offer a coherent explanation of the train of events which has led us into the conditions of pathological labour market failure in which we now find ourselves.

For pathological it certainly is. The Live Register of Unemployed is now roughly 300,000, corresponding to almost 20 per cent of the estimated labour force. There is no country with which Ireland can reasonably be compared which has such a high unemployment rate, and those countries regard their unemployment levels as unacceptable. But the current labour market crisis in Ireland is also new by our own standards. It is not that long since the then Taoiseach, Jack Lynch, acknowledged that his Government deserved to lose office if unemployment went above 100,000. In the 1960s, unemployment was usually around 60,000– 70,000, less than a quarter of today's figure. But by our own historical standards, and by contemporary international comparisons, the labour market position in the Ireland of 1993 stands out like a sore thumb. We have done far better in the past, and other comparable countries are doing better today.

What went wrong? Some of the election manifestoes and political speeches would lead one to believe that it is just an inherent problem, like the Irish weather, something for which no one is to blame. The absence of an examination of how the current situation came about is mute acceptance that high unemployment is a product of fate, a legacy of history; or a handicap of geography, as the fashionable fetish about peripherality would have us believe.

It is, of course, none of these things. Countries in all kinds of historical, geographic, demographic and political circumstances have achieved far lower rates of unemployment than currently obtain in Ireland. The problem is essentially man-made, a progressive failure of economic policy which has been building up for almost two decades. It has been exacerbated by other factors, including technological developments, demographic pressures and unfavourable patterns of change in the external trading environment. But all countries have to face technological change and the other factors are certainly not unique to Ireland.

If bad economic policy is the source of the unemployment crisis, the first step in addressing the issue is to admit, with maximum candour, that this is the case. An admission of error, a *mea culpa*, a plea for forgiveness, and a firm purpose of amendment are perhaps too much to expect in election manifestoes, but in this aspect of Irish economic policy, nothing else would have been appropriate.

There is no example, to my knowledge, of a country in comparable circumstances which has done worse than we have in terms of the balance of supply and demand in the labour market. To deal with the peripherality issue head on, Portugal has an unemployment rate of 8 per cent at the moment. Scotland, in so many ways the most appropriate comparator for Ireland, has just under 10 per cent. Unemployment in the Republic has trebled since 1980. We always had a higher unemployment rate than the United Kingdom. But even here, there is no solace for those who wish to avoid a made-in-Ireland explanation for what has happened. Unemployment here has broken out of its traditional relationship with UK unemployment rates, and is now well above the traditional differential vis-à-vis Britain.

What has gone wrong is very simple at the economic level, and very complex in terms of the politics, and political culture, of the Republic of Ireland. At the economic level, policy has been directed at exaggerating the natural incentives for employers, which are always present, to minimise the numbers employed in economic activity. Simultaneously, the incentives to seek and accept job offers have been weakened. Coinciding with these developments has been a weakening in the attractiveness of traditional outlets for emigrants from Ireland. There has been a kind of ratchet effect operating on economic policy: each rise in unemployment as a result of mistaken policies has triggered an intensification of the same policies. The election manifestoes of November 1992 contained numerous examples of job-creation incentives, fuelled by fresh Exchequer borrowing, which would fall into this category.

The burden of any thesis which says that current policies have created unemployment, and have been doing so for almost two decades, is that no solution is possible unless current policies are abandoned. So what are the elements in current policies which have done most to worsen the unemployment situation? The culprits can be grouped under a number of headings: (1) Taxation Policies; (2) Social Welfare Policies; (3) Labour Market Policies; and (4) Public Sector Waste. There have been developments in all four areas over the last two decades, and on a substantial scale, which, in my view, are the cause of the unemployment crisis. The reversal of policy in all four areas must, it follows, be top of the list in any rational approach to reducing the dole queues.

In the taxation area, we have progressively included workers on lower and lower real incomes in the tax net, for both income tax and the rising burden of PRSI. In the 1960s, workers in the lower-paid brackets were, by and large, outside the tax net. At present, single people earning as little as one-third of the national average wage are liable to pay income tax (at 27 per cent, on top of PRSI and associated payments, the total being 35 per cent). It is one of the greatest ironies in the history of Irish economic policy that the ICTU, the great defenders of the PAYE worker, were vocal supporters of the introduction of PAYE back in the early 1960s. At that time, only higher income earners were liable to income tax. The trades unions saw PAYE as essentially a collection device, which would speed and streamline tax receipts from the better off. The genie released from that particular bottle has played an important role in making unemployment worse. A substantial portion of tax revenue in Ireland now comes from lower income workers, since the basic allowance for PAYE is now so low, lower than the weekly wage of even the most unskilled employee. Indeed, unskilled, part-time workers can even find themselves paying income tax.

This situation has been gravely exacerbated by the introduction of Pay Related Social Insurance in the late 1960s. Politicians have been quite unable to resist the temptation to raise the rates of tax, and PRSI is a tax, and have also added various additional levies. The result is that every employee must now pay almost 8 per cent of income in this form of income tax, without any basic allowance whatsoever.

As a further twist, incomes above a certain limit are not liable, so that the top end of the income distribution is exempt. Most public servants are also exempt, or pay a reduced rate. This group of employees enjoys higher average gross pay and better conditions than the rest of the economy. It would be difficult to design a more regressive form of taxation of workers' incomes than the Irish PRSI system. It has the feature, in both employers' and employees' versions, that higher incomes get off lightly. The employers' rate of PRSI, plus the employees' rate, add up to 20 per cent of gross income in total. There are no basic allowances against either. But the exemption of higher incomes from virtually all of this levy means that the payroll tax on highly skilled workers is far lower, in percentage terms, than the payroll tax on unskilled workers. Between employers' and employees' levies, it works out at about 10 per cent on a £40,000 salary, but at 20 per cent on a £200 a week pay packet. In a country where unemployment is concentrated amongst the less skilled, this is an Alice-in-Wonderland policy.

The social welfare system creates problems for labour market balance in other ways too. The entitlement to various social benefits, for example, medical cards, is linked far too closely to Live Register status. It may be reasonable to target certain entitlements, to ensure that those on high incomes do not qualify, but Live Register status is not an infallible proxy for income, particularly at the household level. It would be far better to work towards a universal means test for all benefits, based on net income from all sources. If this involved the withdrawal of benefit from some households on the grounds that their means exceed the limit, then that is no more than an admission that the entitlement rules have been badly designed and maladministered in the past.

There is the further difficulty with the system that social welfare payments in Ireland are not liable to tax. Someone who receives £100 a week from the social welfare system pays no tax. A single person with no extra allowances earning £100 a week could pay up to £18 in deductions. There are additional expenses in the form of travel to work, which are not tax deductible, and which reduce further the position of the low-paid worker as against the person on social welfare. The use of gross, rather than net, income in assessing means for certain social benefits compounds the distortion. The low-paid worker on an equivalent net income to a social welfare recipient will be entitled to fewer such benefits because of the assessment method used.

There is a conflict here which is perhaps more a question of economics versus social justice than it is a conflict between alternative approaches to rules and regulations in the tax and social welfare system. The labour market will not work effectively if the less-skilled section of the labour force is faced with a situation where work and dole offer much the same net income. Other things being equal, those at work should be better off than those out of work, as a matter of economics. But as a matter of social justice, many Irish people seem to find this difficult to accept. Our current policies appear to me to have surrendered to this difficulty.

The third area in which our policies have moved in a direction which has worsened the unemployment situation is in the various pieces of legislation which have been enacted aimed at protecting the rights of employees. This process commenced in the late 1960s with the Redundancy Payments Act, and has continued through legislation conferring protection against unfair dismissal, rights and entitlements for part-time workers and various other measures. The net effect of these measures is to add to the cost of employing people. This is particularly clear in the case of the redundancy arrangements, where employers must be conscious that taking on new workers involves a contingent liability for payments, over and above the wage bill, if things go badly. All of the other measures impose actual or perceived costs for employers, and perception can be a potent disincentive too. Ireland now has more pro-employee rights legislation than was ever on the statute book in the UK, even under Labour Governments. Large redundancy payouts, for example, are unknown in Britain and employers there can, with greater equanimity, contemplate failure and the need to lay off staff. At a superficial level, everyone is in favour of job security, big payments if you get laid off and any other rights for employees one can think of. The problem is that these rights are no good to the unemployed and they reduce the incentive to employ people. There is a trade-off to be faced.

The final area in which the quality of economic policy in Ireland has worsened in the last two decades, in a fashion which militates against employment growth, is the inexorable growth in public expenditure and the weakening system of control over that growth. There have been very brief interceptions, such as the 1987–9 period, in this Rake's

Progress. The media have played a particularly unhelpful role in this area in the last few years, devoting acres of column inches and æons of air-time to cuts in public spending which have not taken place. The real volume of health spending has grown rapidly in the last few years, which will come as a surprise to some readers, I am sure. Every extra £1 million devoted to public spending is a £1 million which must be raised in taxes. Taxes are ultimately paid by the non-government sector of the economy, since you cannot impose levies on your own spending. Taxes on the non-government sector go straight to overhead, and reduce the competitiveness of that sector. This is a vitally important consideration where the non-government sector is so exposed to international competition.

The waste of public funds takes many forms, but the two most important are: firstly, doing things that simply do not need to be done, and secondly, doing things that do need to be done at too high a cost. Readers can supply their own examples of each. There are quite extraordinary difficulties in Ireland in achieving political agreement on cutting out waste. I have rarely met a politician who does not agree that there is plenty of waste to be cut. But, for each area of waste there is a group of beneficiaries, and the Irish political system, with its intense competition between parties, and the multi-member PR system, gives an inordinate degree of political power to even very small pressure groups. The small size of the country and the intimacy of its political culture are no help either.

However, waste can be cut out, given the political conviction. During the 1987–9 period, state agencies and programmes were dropped which most people could not even name a few years later. The control of public spending is particularly important in the years immediately ahead, since any programme seriously targeted to address the unemployment problem must release the resources to cut sharply the level of taxes on low-income workers. A continued failure to control spending will make it impossible to implement this central reform.

Before considering in a little detail the kinds of policies which are necessary in order to reverse the losses in the labour market, I would like to devote a few moments to some aspects of unemployment which receive limited attention. The first relates to emigration. The United Kingdom remains the destination for 80 per cent of Irish emigrants. In the 1960s, the welfare state system in the UK was far superior to the situation in the Republic and Irish people who had emigrated to Britain had few incentives to come home if things went wrong. The very sharp reversal in emigration flows between the two countries since the onset of the labour market shake-out in the UK in 1990 is, in part, testament to the fact that our welfare state provisions have caught up and that recent emigrants who lose their jobs are more likely to return to Ireland. There are other factors. For example, Ireland has fewer lifestyle restrictions than was the case in the 1960s, and travel is far cheaper in real terms. The recent sharp rise in registered unemployed here is partly due to this factor.

The second aspect is the superimposition on the unemployment problem, which is nationwide, of a specifically urban set of problems which are most noticeable and pronounced in the cities of Dublin and Cork. It has long been an unspoken assumption of Irish policies that the cities are rich and the countryside deprived. This had some validity in the 1960s but has none today. The area of Ireland which has lost most population over that period is not Leitrim or Roscommon, but the city of Dublin. Cork and Dublin have lost most jobs in traditional manufacturing, many of them less-skilled jobs which match the profile of the unemployed. Government has consciously promoted industrial development outside the country's two major cities and with considerable superficial success. But the unemployment problem in the cities has been compounded thereby. Add a misguided public housing policy and you end up with a situation in which the greatest concentration of economic and social deprivation in the country is now to be found in the northern and western suburbs of Dublin and on the north side of

Cork city. These suburbs, many of them bigger than the larger provincial towns, lead the country in unemployment rates, and also in crime, drug abuse, single parent families and all the other symptoms of social breakdown. Some west Dublin suburbs, which had the lowest turnout rates in the country at the last election, also have the lowest rates of church attendance, according to a clerical friend. Ireland now has an urban crisis which is linked to, but broader than, the unemployment crisis. We have, of course, no urban policy, not even an identifiable government department or agency whose responsibility it might be to develop one. What we do have in abundance are policies which are a throwback to the 1960s: decentralising public service jobs to country towns with lower unemployment rates than Dublin, or beggar-my-neighbour political strokes like the Shannon stopover. This emerging urban crisis looks set fair, to this observer, to become a new and challenging issue for Irish national politics in the years immediately ahead.

I want to conclude with an outline of the kinds of policy which we need to pursue if unemployment in Ireland is to be reduced. But first, there are approaches which should be firmly ruled out. Borrowing more money for job-creation schemes is likely to make things worse. Infrastructure either makes sense on its merits or it does not. Borrowing money to finance uneconomic projects is a formula for national impoverishment, as the sorry record since 1977 demonstrates. Make-work schemes and other stunts to reduce the recorded Live Register are just an evasion. Creating unnecessary 'jobs' in the public sector, which must be financed either through higher taxes or higher public sector charges, will only reduce available spending power, and hence employment, in the private economy.

The most important, and most difficult, reform which needs to be undertaken is to stop levying high taxes on low incomes. Not, in my view, to cut top tax rates, which are no longer punitive. It does not make sense, in terms of getting the labour market to work, to seek taxes from people whose gross income from work may be little better than social welfare entitlements. The cost of getting the basic personal allowance in the tax code up to any reasonable relationship with average wages is enormous. The options in financing such a move include an end to exclusively middle-class subsidy programmes, such as mortgage interest relief, VHI relief, and higher education subsidies, the re-introduction of rates on residential property, and across-the-board economies in public spending.

There is also a need to make all income liable to tax on a common basis, and to integrate PRSI into the income tax code, which means an end to the income ceilings for both employers and employees. Of course, PRSI, when integrated into the income tax system, would extend automatically to workers currently exempt. In the social welfare system the status of being unemployed should not bring with it automatic entitlement to other benefits. These should depend on a means test which is universal, wherever a means test is appropriate, and based on net income.

❧ If it is not easy to shed labour, employers will be reluctant to hire people. To pretend otherwise is to deny that Ireland has a market economy. Our labour laws should acknowledge that job creation is a priority. The measures which I have outlined would make labour cheaper to the employer in the lower-skilled areas where unemployment is heaviest. It would help if capital grants and subsidies were reduced further, continuing the process commenced in the mid-1980s, and if the Culliton Committee's approach to industrial policy were pursued. ❧

The policies on the tax, welfare and expenditure control areas which I believe necessary are radical and involve an admission that much of what has been done in the last 20 years was mistaken, however well-intentioned. Radical policy changes are not common in Irish politics, although there was no lack of radicalism in the 1950s and 1960s. Our political culture is increasingly dominated by the preservation of the interests of producer groups – farmers, trades unions, business interests who are recipients of state largesse or protection. The rhetoric of politicians, of all parties, is different;

concern for the unemployed the universal refrain. But the policy consensus includes things like more mortgage interest relief, more subsidies for higher education, more job security in state-owned companies. None of these policies will help the job market, and all of them are socially regressive. The interests of the unemployed – a freer labour market, with tax and welfare reform and less job protection, make it easier for the unemployed to compete with the employed. There has been a movement in politics, it seems to me, away from the representation of the voter as voter and toward the representation of the voter as the member of this or that interest or pressure group. Even the trades unions seem to have drifted away from social democracy, except for rhetorical purposes, and towards a corporatist hegemony of labour market insiders, also known as the social partners. The support of the unions for the revaluation of the currency in the last few months of 1992, against the unprecedented unemployment background, was striking evidence of how far the Irish unions have moved away from their industrial base.

To conclude, the word 'change' was the most over-used of the 1992 general election, as it had been of the American election. But, despite the damage being done by unemployment to the fabric of Irish society, the change in economic policies needed to address the unemployment crisis may have to wait. Wait for change, not just in the personnel of government, but in the nature of the political culture of modern Ireland.

2. The Failure of Failure

Fintan O'Toole

ON THE LAST day, when the Four Horsemen of the Apocalypse come riding down O'Connell Street in all their terrible glory, there will still be a group of unemployed Irish people standing at a bus-stop, waiting to go to the dole office and join the queue. They will look up from their racing pages at the harbingers of doom. One will look at the others and say, 'That's horsemen of the apocalypse all over for you. You wait a millennium for one, and then four come along together.'

We have, in other words, become strangely blasé about the doom of perpetual unemployment. By a strange mixture of historic flaws and recent fashions, we have produced a political culture that is remarkably at home with the idea of mass unemployment and remarkably pessimistic about the prospects of doing anything about it. The fatalism that is apparently endemic in Irish culture has blended with the New Right's scepticism about the power of government, to produce a politics in which there is little real belief that unemployment can be tackled.

The contemporary Irish economy did not emerge out of nowhere. Ireland came into the global economy in the 1960s out of a context shaped by Catholicism and nationalism. The transformation shaped by Lemass and Whitaker was so immediately successful that it was easy to forget that it came on top of, and not instead of, a society that was still shaped by famine and trauma. The sense that we would never know a poor day again obliterated the poor days that we had known. Dazzled by the new optimism, we forgot that our underlying faith was one in which the world was a vale of tears, that our underlying politics was one which had coined the phrase 'The Triumph of Failure'.

The economic optimism arising from the 1960s greeted mass unemployment in the 1970s with outrage and urgency. Lemass' heir, Jack Lynch, said that if unemployment reached 100,000, the Taoiseach should resign. Fianna Fáil in 1977 launched a political and economic manifesto whose essential slogan was 'Keynes Means Beans'. The failure of that manifesto was not a mere case of a short-term policy that didn't work. It became the failure of a philosophy of government. Ireland's brief experiment with activist government discredited the very idea of activist government. Instead of seeing that failure as a tragedy, we chose to see it as a farce and the bitter laughter is echoing through our politics still. The 1960s of Lemass and Whitaker ended for us in 1979: a long Easter Sunday of economic resurrection followed by a long Good Friday of grim fatalism.

That fatalism had remained strong in our culture, but had been masked by the optimism let loose by Lemass and Whitaker. It is partly the result of having such a religious culture, one which is inevitably prone to seeing this world and its troubles as temporary but irredeemable, and to seeing suffering as innately noble. It is also partly the result of a political culture whose governing narrative has been one of glorious failure.

In the 1980s, however, there was a new form for these old impulses to assume. The economic orthodoxies of the New Right provided the new bottles for the old wine. Our failure to create a stable society was endorsed by the New Right's view that there was no such thing as society anyway. Our sense that Irish Governments had failed to create jobs was endorsed by the New Right's view that governments not merely could not, but should not, create jobs. Ivor Kenny, one of the most articulate analysts of Irish economic culture from a right-wing perspective, quoted with approval Ronald Reagan's statement that 'in this present crisis, government is not the solution, it is the problem'. Our sense that government was powerless was endorsed by the New Right view that it should be powerless. Mrs Thatcher's return to Victorian values was, in its Irish form, a return to Famine values, to the fatalism that overtakes a society that has reason to be grateful for small mercies.

A Malthusian pessimism that would not have been out of place in Victorian times, became part of Irish political rhetoric after the mid 1980s, as the most dramatic consequence of unemployment, the return to mass emigration, took hold. Brian Lenihan, one of the best attuned of political antennae, picked up the mood when he explained emigration by saying that 'we can't all live on a small island'. A new vision of our economic and political failure to create jobs as a natural, biological and even geographical one was conjured up. For most of the last five years, the explanation for unemployment has been essentially Malthusian: we are breeding too fast, there are too many young people coming on the labour market. It was a vision still deeply marked by the fear of famine, of a population breeding beyond the capacity of its economic resources to sustain it.

Brian Lenihan himself gave perhaps the best indicator of this slightly surreal use of famine imagery in a 1990s high-tech world, during the last election campaign, when he spoke of the fact that 'the state is not here to provide jobs', and put Irish historic emigration, the result of famine, in a context that made it sound like a post-modern celebration of the global village:

> If someone is trained and educated and they make their way in life somewhere else, good. We've done our job. We're living in a globe, you know, we're living in one big village ... I've no hang-up about this, I'm part of the world family. I believe the Irish are a great world race. I'm very proud of that. That's a philosophy I have.

In this line of thought, a fundamental pessimism about the role of the state in job creation is married to a sense of Ireland as both an ultra-modern and a post-famine society. That conjunction, strange as it may seem at first glance, is an accurate reflection of a situation in which despair about jobs is fuelled by both New Right influence and Irish historical and religious fatalism.

This, however, is not the only paradox that affects our response to the jobs crisis. The essential contradiction is that, while on the one hand we distrust the capacity of the state to create jobs, the consequence of this distrust is, in fact, a huge level of state activity and expenditure on job creation. We spend as much as any comparable society on job creation, but we do so in order to create the 'climate' for jobs, not jobs themselves.

What we have created in Ireland is neither a minimalist laissez faire state on the one hand, nor a truly activist state on the other. The *First Programme for Economic Expansion* set the tone for this curious contradiction. Itself the greatest example of state intervention in the history of Irish job creation policy, it is also extraordinarily modest in its aims, seeing its own role as merely the stimulation of private enterprise. 'There is,' it says, 'no substitute for private enterprise, and the main objective of government policy in this field is to create the conditions in which it will be stimulated'. The *Second Programme for Economic Expansion* copper-fastened this logic: the ultimate aim is job creation, but the immediate objectives are 'higher productivity and greater competitiveness'.

This paradox is important if we are to understand the present crisis. We have tended to contrast the success of job creation in the 1960s with its failure in the 1980s and 1990s. In reality, one is the obverse side of the other. The success of the 1960s was achieved essentially by a ceding of state control over the economy, in terms of the withdrawal of tariff barriers and protectionist policies. It was also a stepping back from national control – depending as it did on foreign multinational investment. In a sense, the state was most successful at creating jobs when it took its heavy hand off the tiller. Because it worked, we became hooked on the idea that less is more, that the less actual control over the economy we had, the more powerful the state became at creating jobs. This metaphysical conceit of a state that should be extremely active in planning and investing, but extremely powerless in actually ensuring that the investment and planning had their desired effect – jobs – appealed to both the activism of the times and the fatalism of the underlying culture.

It became so much the norm here that we forget that it is not the norm in those late-developing countries which successfully industrialised themselves and created close to full employment in the process. In Japan, or Taiwan or South Korea, industrial growth was led by a state which was much more active in direct job creation and in shaping the free market than the Irish state has been.

The very success of the Irish experiment in the 1960s and 1970s, though, has led to the failure of the 1980s and 1990s. The loss of state control and the acceptance of state powerlessness, combined with the very high level of state expenditure on job creation – a policy of 'give the money and run' – is precisely the formula that has led to our present dilemma.

The indirect notion of job creation on which we founded our 1960s economic miracle – create the conditions and the jobs will follow – worked well in the short term, but badly in the long term. Jobs are always the end of a process that can never quite be completed. Much of the last decade in Irish economic orthodoxy has been a succession of prescriptions for changing the economic climate that have been about as successful as rain dances or sacrifices to the sun god might be in changing the physical climate. Increase competitiveness and jobs will follow. Control wages and jobs will follow. Increase confidence and jobs will follow. Boost exports and jobs will follow. Reduce inflation and jobs will follow. We have done it all, and the jobs have not followed. There has been a complete disjunction between cause and effect, in which the causes have had no effects, only consequences. The paradox of an activist but powerless state has given us the even more unpleasant paradox of a successful economy but an extremely unsuccessful society.

The fatal flaw which means that any simplistic idea of cause and effect cannot work for job creation in Ireland is, of course, that the Irish economy is not in any sense a closed system. It is an extremely open system in which many of the crucial factors — the repatriation of profits, the fictional nature of export figures because of large scale transfer pricing by multinational companies – are literally unknown. The climatological school of economics is like an attempt to apply Newtonian physics in an Einsteinian universe. It is a pretence that Ireland is a place where simple laws of cause and effect can be applied to a massive economic and political task like job creation. If the laws of gravity work, the apple will fall on your head. If the laws of the market are allowed to work, the jobs will fall into our laps. The problem is that the Irish economy isn't like that. It has its own laws of relativity, its own bending light beams, its own space-time singularities, and, of course, its own Black Hole, the economists' apt description of the phenomenon whereby much of our GNP disappears in the form of repatriated profits. Working in the dark as they are, it is hardly surprising that our weathermen of the climatological school have never been very good at knowing which way the wind is blowing.

In a sense, before we can start to talk seriously about job creation, we have to address two other things. One is the role of the state itself. The other is the broader culture of fatalism which inhibits our notion of that role. Unless we believe that change can happen, and that the state can make it happen, then there is little point in talking about job creation policy at all.

The general pessimism about the ability of the state to do anything substantial about jobs is partly a political mechanism and partly a reflection of the reality of the Irish state as it has, in fact, developed. The political side is, to some degree, ideological, but, perhaps to a larger degree, pragmatic. The notion that the state can't or shouldn't be responsible for creating jobs is a respectable ideological position. But it is also a handy way out. It means that there is no-one to blame. Like the 'Act of God' clauses in insurance policies, it accounts for a mysterious process which either works or doesn't, in the same way that Nature carries out its mysterious handiwork. Ultimately, politicians are no more to blame for the economic and employment climate than they are for the real natural climate. A rise in unemployment is no more the subject of political responsibility than a heavy snowfall or a miserable downpour. Conversely, if politicians really believed that they could solve the problem, they would not be so keen on a philosophy which gives the praise to the obscure workings of the economic climate.

However, it would be wrong not to acknowledge that the notion that the state is incapable of creating jobs does have a real basis in the kind of state we have created. We created a paradoxical kind of state: one that, especially since the 1970s, channels a massive amount of the gross national product but manages very little of it. Because of high taxation and a highly centralised system of government, a great deal of the national wealth passes through state hands. But because of the ramshackle nature of that state, the creaking mechanism of theoretical ministerial responsibility and semi-autonomous state companies and institutions, combined with the ideology of a hands-off state, this somewhat bloated body has never been able to use its limbs effectively. We have given the state great power but little responsibility. As the authors of *Understanding Contemporary Ireland*[1] have put it, 'increased public expenditure is not to be confused with increased state management'. We have had the worst of both worlds – massive state involvement in the economy, but with consequences that are unintended and uncontrolled.

This deep sense of powerlessness was starkly illustrated in the 1992 general election campaign. The two main parties showed clearly that they had deep doubts about the capacity of the state really to deal with a situation in which around 25,000 jobs a year must be created merely to stand still at crisis levels of unemployment. Fine Gael's central job creation mechanism was a direct reduction in the state's involvement, a cut in employers' PRSI which it was hoped would provide an incentive to employers. It was a classic 'less is more' formula. Fianna Fáil, on the other hand, proposed a moderately interventionist solution, but its lack of faith in it was amply demonstrated when its leader, Mr Reynolds, was asked at the party's manifesto launch how many jobs it would create and replied that he didn't want to say because if he did no one would believe him. That answer, in its painful honesty, betrayed better than anything the almost unconscious loss of faith at the heart of the system, the sense of despair about convincing itself, never mind the general public, of the state's capacity to affect things.

Because of this despair, any real attempt to tackle the jobs crisis has to go hand in hand with a thorough reform of the system of government itself. A more efficient, rational, and therefore more open and democratic system of government is a prerequisite to a state which can be effective in tackling a national emergency like the one in which we now find ourselves. A part of that system must be a forum in which those who suffer most from unemployment – the unemployed themselves – are given a real voice and real power. That the demands of the unemployed for a Jobs Forum have been met only by the establishment of a committee of a patently ineffective Oireachtas is as much a symptom of the problem as a solution to it. A system of government in which those who suffer the consequences of economic failures remain remote from those who bear much of the blame for those failures, is precisely a system from which we have to move away. Without an open, participative and highly critical system of government, we will not have a credible state. And a state that is not credible has little chance of providing the coherent leadership which is needed for the kind of effort we have to envisage if the problem is to be contained, let alone solved.

Assuming that such a thorough structural reform can begin, the next step is a move to create a limited but substantial number of jobs directly by the state. Even accepting that direct state job creation in the public service is a dangerous and possibly counter-productive move on the basis of the 1977 Manifesto experience, it is wrong to conclude that it has no role at all. The consequences of such a move are dangerous only if it leads to a permanent and absolute increase in the level of state spending, requiring a large increase in borrowing. If, however, such jobs are created specifically for people who are already unemployed, involving a direct addition to what they already earn on social welfare to bring their income up to an acceptable level, then the amount of extra expenditure by the state is limited and the jobs exist only so long as the unemployment crisis does. The parties of the left proposed at the end of 1992 that 25,000 such jobs could be provided full-time and a further 25,000 part-time, and there would seem to be no reason why this could not be done within a responsible limit on state borrowing.

This would have two immediate effects. Firstly, it would help to break the cycle of despair, demonstrating that the state does have the capacity in the short term to create jobs. Secondly, it would attack the terrible hold of a social welfare system that condemns so many people to a stultified dependency, in which there is no middle way between complete redundancy on the one hand and gainful employment on the other. Contrary to the orthodoxy which holds that we need to create a clear dividing line between social welfare recipients and workers, in order to provide a mythical 'incentive to work', the need is, in fact, to blur the distinction between employment and unemployment by allowing those who are drawing the dole to work as often as they can without necessarily losing their benefits. Ways of combining social welfare benefit and earned income have to be devised in order to free the great untapped economic resource represented by the unemployed and to generate some economic activity from the £3.5 billion a year we spend on social welfare.

Hand in hand with these steps to improve the credibility of the state, and to demonstrate its capacity for direct action, there has to be also a somewhat paradoxical recognition that change has to be effected at levels both lower and higher than the state. What I mean is that we have to recognise, as we have not done to any sufficient extent, that the world we now inhabit is one in which the state itself has to act as a bridge between the local and the supranational, between the communities that make up the country and the European Community of which the country is a part. On the one hand, we have to unleash the power of local communities to create jobs, while, on the other hand, recognising that only at an EC level are we capable of influencing global forces and trans-national corporations that control our economic destinies.

Because of its small size, relative cultural homogeneity, and relatively intact sense of social solidarity, you would expect Ireland to be at the forefront of developing new and imaginative ways of allowing local communities to con-tribute to the solution of their unemployment problems. The reality is otherwise. It is striking that most state funding for such community development programmes as there are – an average of £50,000 a year for each project – comes through the Department of Social Welfare rather than Industry and Commerce. It is seen as a palliative rather than as a resource for development. And most of that funding, in turn, has its source in the National Lottery, marking it as a frill, an op-tional luxury.

Some promising developments took place in 1992, with the establishment under the Programme for Economic and Social Progress of area-based initiatives for tackling long-term unemployment, and the related decision to establish County Enterprise Partnership Boards. But these ideas have so far been funded in a way that speaks volumes about the level of real importance which is given to them. Bursaries to allow local development workers to be trained were allo-cated all of £20,000 in the 1992 Budget. The Department of Social Welfare's grant scheme for local women's groups, often the core of development in disadvantaged commu-nities, had a budget of £500,000 in 1992. Every group is funded on a one-off basis, with no guarantee that it will be funded for more than a year. The mentality is one of hand-outs and sops, not of serious efforts to allow local communities the resources to begin to formulate solutions to unemployment at their own level.

The Community Action Network, which represents most of the community-based groups, has pointed out that it is often only when they are fronted by a priest that local groups are successful in getting state funds because 'the state accepts the role of religious as legitimising the work being undertaken'. To put it more bluntly, local initiatives remain, as far as the state is concerned, in the category of religious good works and alms for the poor, not that of serious solutions to unemployment.

The communities in which long-term unemployment is concentrated have to be allowed to break out of their marginalisation and powerlessness if that unemployment is to be tackled. Yet the Irish state is too often a dog in the manger, snapping at any gifts of gold, frankincense and myrrh which might be offered to such communities. The National Development Plan which was put to the EC for the use of structural funds was drawn up without any real consultation with community groups. And an offer of £8 million from the European Commission was actually refused by the Government because the Commission required that it be administered by local groups and not by central government. This negative and patronising attitude often means that community enterprise schemes can be counter-productive. The most extensive report of community action – Mary Whelan and Patricia Kelleher's *Dublin Communities In Action*,[2] published in 1992 – finds that many enterprise schemes generate a 'sense of failure and frustration at individual and community level' by promising what they cannot deliver. The rhetoric of allowing people to stand on their own two feet is in practice translated into a system which steps on the toes of those who do.

This attitude can be changed and changed quickly, since it is entirely within the power of the Irish political system to do so. What is not within the power of the Irish political system is an adequate response to the global forces and transnational corporations which determine so much of the power of the Irish state to create jobs. Ironically, while the Irish State treats its marginalised communities as troublesome children, Ireland itself is, in the EC context, a marginalised community within the Community. We belong to the 40 per cent of the EC's land area that has just 20 per cent of the population and 13 per cent of the Gross Domestic Product. Our level of access to the EC's markets is 55 per cent of the EC average. We are, in other words, a poor, marginalised suburb of the EC.

It is all the more remarkable, therefore, that our industrial policy has been largely unaffected by EC membership. As economists have pointed out, our industrial policy has been altered very little by 20 years of EC membership, partly because EC industrial policy has been desperately weak and partly because the essential aim of ours has been the attraction of largely non-EC multinationals. What has happened at EC level has been hugely important to us, of course, but its aims have been largely negative – preventing barriers to internal trade, preventing unfair competition – rather than positive.

If we are to get out of the present crisis, we need the EC to develop a dynamic industrial policy. But in order to be able to argue for that, we need to show that we practise what we preach. If we want to be listened to, we need to start listening. If we want urgent action, we need to show urgency. If we want positive intervention into the free play of market forces in Europe, we need to begin it at home. We need to set out with a sober optimism, aware of the depth of our difficulties, but genuinely convinced that they can be overcome.

Footnotes

[1] Richard Breen, Damian F. Hannan, David B. Rottman, Christopher T. Whelan, *Understanding Contemporary Ireland*, Gill and Macmillan, Dublin, 1990.

[2] Patricia Kelleher and Mary Whelan, *Dublin Communities in Action*, Community Action Network and Combat Poverty Agency, Dublin, 1992.

3. Growth and Jobs:
The Politics of Public Ambivalence

Dr Garret FitzGerald

THAT PUBLIC POLICY has made unemployment worse than it need have been in Ireland is undeniable. However, this is not the whole story. For, no matter what policies had been pursued, unemployment in Ireland would in any event today have been at a high level.

It is necessary right at the outset to get this fact straight and not to be misled into thinking that all our unemployment is somehow our own fault. Otherwise we face a double risk – of undue pessimism on the one hand, through an exaggeration of our own past failures, or on the other hand undue optimism through misleading ourselves into thinking that all we need to do to solve the entire problem is, belatedly, to change mistaken policies.

I'd like in this paper to pinpoint more precisely *why* unemployment is so high and, above all, to identify the extent to which its level may – or may *not* – be attributable to a particular Irish failure to generate new jobs. Next, I would like to examine how we might accelerate the growth of employment so as to reduce the number out of work, and, to the extent that there is such a failure, to discuss the nature of some of the impediments to such an acceleration of employment growth. Finally, I want to advert to the manner in which politicians in power have been, and still are, inhibited from tackling these impediments to job creation by the political pressures that emanate from those – the great majority of voters – who are lucky enough to have a job and a level of purchasing power that they want to preserve and enhance.

FIRST – the reasons why unemployment is so high today. A major negative influence on our employment performance in the latter part of the 1970s and early 1980s was the general slowing down of growth, especially in Western Europe, in the decade after the first oil crisis. This culminated in virtual economic stagnation between 1979 and 1983, which almost doubled European unemployment. To a much greater extent than is generally appreciated, *our* poor employment performance in these years reflected this general pattern, costing us probably some 75,000 jobs.

Between 1983 and 1990 there was, however, a recovery in economic growth world-wide; in Western Europe as a whole employment rose by about 10 per cent and unemployment declined slightly. Yet in Ireland in these years employment recorded no net increase, and despite emigration of almost 200,000, unemployment in 1990, after some fluctuations, was at about the same level as it had been seven years earlier – and has since risen by a further 50,000.

Why has our experience since 1983 been so different from that of the rest of Western Europe? A major part of the explanation for this lies in the fact that during the 1970s the number of births had risen steadily in Ireland while the birth rate elsewhere was falling, so that by 1980 our birth rate was 75 per cent higher than in the rest of Western Europe. This meant that while in the rest of Western Europe the number of young people seeking employment having completed their education was falling – very rapidly indeed in some countries like Germany – in Ireland the number of potential job-seekers was increasing.

It is worth reflecting for a moment on just why the number of births here rose in the 1970s by almost one-fifth. The reason was that from the early 1960s onwards accelerated economic growth had brought about a quite rapid rise in employment in Ireland outside agriculture, and a decline in emigration. The young people who got these new jobs soon got married, more than doubling the young married population before the end of the 1970s. When this marriage boom began, artificial contraception, initially in the form of the pill, was only starting to gain ground. It was not until 1980 that the decline in fertility, as a result of the belated spread of contraception, began to outweigh the impact on the birth rate of that huge increase in the young married population.

The expansion of employment during the 1970s was such, indeed, that some 25,000 earlier emigrants returned to work in Ireland, bringing with them their spouses, and over 50,000 children, born in Britain, who, as they finished their education, further swelled the numbers who were seeking employment here in the 1980s.

Altogether the effect on our young population – directly, by increasing the number of births (which would otherwise have declined rapidly with the extension of contraception from the mid-1960s onwards), and indirectly as a result of returning emigrants in the 1970s bringing their children with them – has already been to add to our potential job-seekers some 100,000 young people now in their late teens or twenties – with many, many more to come in the years ahead.

Finally, during the past three years the safety valve of emigration has been blocked by the depressed economic conditions in Britain and the United States. The sharp rise in unemployment since 1990 is largely attributable to this factor.

Thus, a significant part of our emigration and unemployment problem today does not derive from recent economic failures at home, but rather from a consequence of past Irish economic success yielding an increase in the flow of young people to the labour market, and from the external economic factor of the slowing down of economic growth in the world during the decade from 1974 to 1983, and more recently as a result of the recession of the early 1990s in Britain and the United States.

Against this background it can be seen that even if we had been much more successful in developing our own economy during the past two decades, we could not have avoided significant emigration and an increase in unemployment over this period. Or, to put it another way: when account is taken of the still growing numbers of young people annually completing their education, as well as the very large number of Irish emigrants of the 1980s who, if jobs were available, would return to Ireland with enthusiasm, and of many married women who would re-enter the labour market if they saw any actual prospect of employment, we should have to achieve an economic growth rate approaching 10 per cent *every* year for the next decade in order both to prevent future emigration *and* at the same time to bring unemployment down to the level of the 1960s and early 1970s. So far as I am aware, no European country has achieved more than a 5 per cent annual growth rate for such a period of time.

Thus, anyone, whether in politics or outside it, who suggests that our unemployment/emigration problem is capable of being *resolved,* as distinct from being mitigated, by any conceivable changes in public policy, is grossly exaggerating the potential role of government action, past or future, in relation to these problems.

HOWEVER, THAT said, it is, of course, true that *part* of the problem *is* of our own making. To start with, despite the undoubted impact of the world recession in the early 1980s, our economic growth in the first half of that decade would not have been quite so slow if it had not been necessary during these years to cut public spending and to raise taxes. This was necessary as part of the process of reducing the totally unsustainable level to which Exchequer borrowing had been raised by extravagant public spending policies in the late 1970s. The lesson of these mistakes has, I believe, been learnt; I doubt if any future Government will ever again try to spend its way to prosperity.

There is, however, a further, subtler, policy issue that is raised by the pattern of our economic performance in the 1980s. While, as had been the case since the mid-1960s, we continued throughout this period to achieve a higher growth rate than in the rest of Western Europe outside the Iberian Peninsula, this growth yielded less and less extra jobs from the mid-1970s onwards. Our output per worker, or labour productivity, which even before then had been rising somewhat faster than in the rest of Western Europe, increased year after year at rates well over twice those of our European neighbours.

There were several reasons for this.

One is that during the 1980s, agriculture, with a declining labour force, increased output sharply, yielding an enormous increase in output per worker – and this sector looms much larger in the Irish economy than in those of other Western European countries.

Another factor, however, was the extent to which the growth of our industrial output and exports after the mid-1970s was in large measure a function of an inflow of new high-tech industries mainly from the United States – most notably electronic, computer, instrument engineering, and pharmaceutical firms. These four industries have all increased their output phenomenally but between them they have provided barely 15,000 extra jobs. By far the greater part of the value added here by high-tech firms in sectors such as these takes the form of profits, the great bulk of which are exported and re-invested elsewhere.

The added value figure for these industries is in any event exaggerated by virtue of the fact that *some* of the profits recorded as being made here are actually profits earned elsewhere but attributed by the firms concerned to this country in order that their eventual retained profits may benefit from our low industrial tax rate. So, a significant part of the extraordinary increase in output per worker in Ireland has really nothing to do with labour productivity and not much to do with value added and retained in Ireland.

That said, it would nevertheless be a mistake to denigrate, as is sometimes done, the very real benefits, in the form of the not inconsiderable number of often highly-paid jobs, that we have derived from the establishment here of industries such as these. For these four sectors – together with one other largely foreign-owned industry, plastics – have between them provided the *only* employment increases in the manufacturing sector during the past decade.

ˋ What *can* be questioned, however, is whether the scale of grants paid by Irish taxpayers in order to attract these particular industries to this country has been fully justified.ˋ For these four predominantly US owned industrial sectors now account for something like half of our industrial output, but they employ barely one-fifth of our manufacturing workforce. And it is fair to ask whether perhaps there might not have been some other way in which part at least of the hundreds of millions of pounds of industrial grants paid to these 150 or so firms could have been deployed differently, so as to provide more than the relatively small figure of about 15,000 additional jobs that have been created in these four sectors.

Of course it's easy to criticise what has been done in terms of industrial policy; it is not easy to be sure, however, that a different approach would necessarily have worked, viz. that if greater efforts had been made to encourage more labour-intensive industries, these would have succeeded – especially given the vulnerability of many such industries to competition from countries with lower pay and tax rates.

This raises the whole question of the role that our pay and tax levels may have had in slowing the growth of employment here.

In relation to employment creation, more attention is usually paid to tax levels than to pay levels – partly, perhaps, because it is popular to advocate lower taxation but unpopular to suggest that the level of pay may affect employment possibilities! I am not, however, convinced that the income tax system – whatever about its equity – is quite as big an obstacle to employment as is sometimes suggested. Nevertheless, before tackling the thorny issue of the relationship between pay and employment, I should, I think, briefly, address the adverse effect of our present tax system on jobs.

A tax system *can* distort the employment market in a

number of different ways. Thus, high corporate taxes can discourage enterprise, and high rates of income tax can at the margin discourage employees from working harder – or can even, in extreme cases, provoke them to move to another country where taxation is less heavy.

Usually taxes are higher in better-off countries, whose citizens can afford to pay more tax while retaining an adequate level of take-home pay. But although in terms of income per head we rate twentieth among twenty-three industrialised countries, international comparisons for the year 1990 showed us ninth in terms of the proportion of the average industrial wage of a single worker absorbed by income tax and social security contributions. And in terms of the proportion of the average industrial wage taken in the case of a married worker with two children, we tied with Germany and New Zealand – two high-income countries – for *third* place amongst these industrialised countries. These figures point to a significantly higher tax take on this level of income than would seem appropriate for a country at our stage of development.

Of even greater significance, perhaps, is the fact that from data it would appear that a single worker on the average industrial wage in Ireland suffers a higher deduction from any *additional* earnings than anywhere else in the industrialised world – 56 per cent taken in tax, leaving the worker with only 44p out of every extra £1 earned. In neighbouring Britain – the most relevant comparison for most Irish workers – the equivalent marginal tax figure was only 34p in the £1, and similar low marginal tax rates applied in the Netherlands, Italy, Spain, Portugal and Japan.

By contrast, because employers' social welfare contributions are lower here than in most other European countries, we are not so much out of line in terms of the proportion of total remuneration that employers here have to deduct for income tax and social welfare contributions.

What these comparisons suggest is that while in international terms our PRSI contributions seem reasonable, we rely excessively on income tax for general revenue – and that our marginal tax rates on many lower level incomes are far too high.

A glance at the tax régimes in other countries indicates that their more favourable income tax levels owe a good deal to the existence there of alternative kinds of taxes that are absent in Ireland – such as local taxes on property, and wealth taxes – as well as higher corporate tax rates. And while our low rate of corporate taxation on manufacturing and on internationally traded services can be justified as an incentive to industrial development, no similar grounds can be advanced for our preference for high income tax rates, with their potentially disincentive effects, as against taxes on property, which have no equivalent negative consequences.

Although the possible negative impact on employment of high *marginal* income tax rates and excessive tax deductions from relatively low incomes has attracted considerable comment for some time past, the income tax reforms of recent years have largely ignored this issue and have perversely been concentrated almost entirely on tax *rates*. In particular since 1989, these reforms have been principally directed towards reducing the top tax rate drastically, from 58 per cent to 48 per cent – which is of course quite irrelevant to the great majority of overtaxed lower-income workers. The Programme for Partnership commits the new Government to a reversal of this policy.

However, if we are serious about jobs, there is an even more important issue than taxation – the level of pay rates. Pay is the price of labour and if the price of anything is too high, demand is depressed.

If an economy were closed, that is if no one could leave it or enter it, and if the bargaining strength of employers and workers were evenly balanced and free from distortions on either side, pay would tend to be at a level that would equate the supply and demand for labour.

In the real world of modern Europe, however, none of these conditions applies. People are free to leave to get jobs elsewhere at higher pay rates, should they wish to do so. Moreover, the bargaining position of employers and workers is not evenly balanced: the smaller number of employers could fairly easily combine to keep wages artificially low – and since the last century, workers have been organised in trades unions to offset this imbalance of potential bargaining power.

Furthermore, on behalf of the community, the state levies taxes to finance public services and to look after those who are not provided for through the pay system – for not everybody is able to work, and many people are not dependents of workers and would, without state help, be destitute. And, as has just been pointed out, the impact of these taxes on employment can distort the market for labour still further, while social welfare payments based on family need may offer people with families a higher living standard if they are unemployed than wages fixed in the marketplace will do.

At the end of the day, all of these factors distort the labour market to an extent that may render totally coincidental any resemblance between the wages paid and the wage rate that would balance the supply of and demand for labour. The existence of a lot of unemployment is at least strong *prima facie* evidence that our pay rates may have been pushed higher than is desirable from an employment viewpoint.

The problem is complicated by the fact that there are marked variations in the balance of the pay-determining forces in different sectors of our economy. Throughout the post-war period workers in the public service have been highly unionised and the trade unions that represent them have tended to favour remuneration being determined by national pay agreements. These public service unions are the dominant forces in a pay bargaining process carried out at that level. By contrast, at the other extreme, workers in the private sector have been much less unionised, and have as a result been able to exert less pressure on the bargaining process. Not surprisingly in these circumstances, our public service pay rates tend to be high vis-à-vis those in neighbouring countries, and women's pay rates in the private sector tend to be relatively low.

The relationship between pay and jobs is easiest to trace in the public sector. The last ten years have seen much job-shedding in public employment as successive Governments have sought to hold down public spending. While some of this job-shedding was fully justified to eliminate feather-bedding, in other cases it has had the effect of cutting back important public services, some of which are now self evidently under-manned. And in such cases it is arithmetically evident that if pay rates had risen less, then the existing sums of money devoted to staffing these services could have been used to employ more people. If the Government and the public service unions had jointly given *absolute* priority to the reduction of unemployment, it would have been open to them to achieve this outcome by negotiating smaller increases in public service pay, or even a pay standstill, in return for an equivalent increase in the number of public service jobs in sectors where there are now many vacancies to be filled.

It is, of course, possible to devise a whole series of arguments against such a deal. For example: why should public service workers have to make such a sacrifice that would not be shared by those in the private sector? Are not many public service workers at the lower end of the pay scales living on incomes that barely match unemployment payments? And would it not be unjust to ask them to make such a sacrifice? And so on. But these are all objections that could be overcome if the will were there to do so. Clearly, that will does not exist, quite simply because, whatever may be claimed to the contrary, reducing unemployment is *not* an absolute priority for most of us who have jobs.

In the private sector the opportunities are, of course, somewhat less clear-cut. First of all, there aren't as many cases as there are in the public sector where firms have vacancies that could be filled without additional investment in premises and in extra machinery and equipment. And even where this could be done, it might be difficult to ensure that, if pay increased more slowly, or even if there were to be a pay standstill, the benefits would accrue to the unemployed in the form of jobs, and would not be used instead by employers simply to increase their profits. Nevertheless, if reducing unemployment *were* the absolute priority, then, with goodwill all around, deals designed to create employment in the private sector could also be worked out in many cases.

The truth is that this whole subject is shot through with public ambivalence and with what I describe as the 'labourers in the vineyard' syndrome. For it would clearly be difficult to organise a 'jobs for pay' exchange on an even-handed nationwide basis – and the instinctive reaction of many of us to a *partial* programme along these lines would be an outraged: 'Why should I make such a sacrifice if others are escaping it?' – just as the labourers in the vineyard resented the payment of the same sum to those who had worked for one hour and to those who had worked for the whole day. Our sense of outrage at not being treated equitably vis-à-vis others is, I am afraid, far stronger than our sense of outrage at injustices suffered by others – in this case the injustice of unemployment.

IN THIS connection, it may be worth reflecting on the experience of some other countries which have had much greater success than we have had in job creation. Two of these are European countries – Portugal and Greece – which have both achieved substantial increases in manufacturing employment in the past two decades, whilst we have recorded no net increase in jobs in this sector over the last 20 years. Moreover, employment in services has risen by three-quarters in both these countries, as against an increase of only one-third in service employment here.

It is, of course, true that both Greece and Portugal are poorer countries than Ireland, being at a somewhat earlier stage of economic development than this country. But may their relative success in employment creation perhaps owe something also to their geographical location, in parts of

Europe where they do not suffer as we do from the proximity of richer neighbours, who in our case, provide a standing temptation to us to aim for standards of public services that are often beyond this country's means, and can be paid for only by excessive borrowing and high taxes? Certainly in both Greece and Portugal taxation has absorbed a smaller proportion of national output than in Ireland, and the average wage is lower than here – very much lower in the case of Portugal.

Another country that has been notably successful in generating jobs in the past 20 years is the United States – where employment has risen four times as fast as in Western Europe. A significant proportion of this increase, although by no means all, has been in low-paid service industries: sectors like catering are not unionised in the United States to the extent they are here. Have we perhaps been so concerned to ensure good wages for our workers that we have inhibited the creation of jobs which, even if low-paid, would be welcome to many young people who are now unemployed here?

I cannot answer the questions raised by the much better employment performance of these three countries. But these are at least issues that deserve more study.

THIS BRINGS me to the final issue I want to address – the fact that politicians have not been prepared to tackle the obstacles to greater employment that are posed by public ambivalence about such issues as tax reform and pay policy. It is here that the operation of the Irish democratic process seems to pose an obstacle to the kind of policies that could make a real impact on unemployment. For action to limit pay increases in the public service or elsewhere, or action to reform our tax system in the way it needs to be reformed would be unpopular with various interest groups. And the almost universal belief of politicians – based on bitter experience – is that where reforms involve shifts in purchasing power, even if these benefit *more* people than they disadvantage, a greater number of votes are lost amongst those hurt by such reforms than are ever won amongst those who benefit financially from them.

A classic example of this was the reaction to the decision of the National Coalition Government in 1974 to replace Death Duties by a 1 per cent Wealth Tax on property with a value in excess of £500,000 in terms of present-day money values. Although the tax liabilities of over 99 per cent of people with any property to leave to their families were in fact *reduced* by this reform, a skilful campaign by some members of this tiny minority of very wealthy people frightened so many of the beneficiaries of this reform into believing that they would also lose by it instead of gaining, that the Opposition of the day was persuaded to promise to abolish this tax when it came to power again. And this they did in 1977, as well as abolishing domestic rates on residential property at the same time.

Fine Gael, for its part, never felt able to face the unpopularity that a restoration of either of these taxes would have entailed. And Labour, when it joined with Fine Gael in Government on two subsequent occasions did not feel that it could reasonably press such an unpopular proposal. In the recent general election indeed, Labour even felt it necessary to promise that, if in Government, it would not re-introduce either property or wealth taxes.

As a result of all this, Ireland since 1977, in contrast to almost all other industrialised countries, has no taxes on the *possession* as distinct from *acquisition* of wealth or property, with the single limited exception of the Residential Property Tax paid by only about 10,000 people who have *both* relatively high incomes and *also* dwellings worth £100,000 or more.

Since this fairly searing political experience of the repercussions of an attempt at a minor improvement in the tax system that would have benefited 199 voters out of every 200, most Irish politicians seem to have lost their stomach for *real* tax reform. And so the features of our tax code that benefit particular groups of taxpayers but discourage entrepreneurs from creating jobs, and workers from taking them, have remained firmly embedded in the system despite the apparent strength of public pressure for action to reduce unemployment.

At the same time, there seems to be little immediate likelihood of action to spread service employment through what might be described as 'pay-sharing', or of extra jobs being created in the private sector by holding wages constant in what is now a period of exceptionally low inflation. For the pressures against any action of this kind that might be really effective in expanding employment have, at least hitherto, been too strong for politicians to contemplate them.

The removal of these obstacles to generating more jobs, and thus at least mitigating the appalling scale of unemployment, would certainly require outstanding political leadership. But so long as public opinion remains deeply ambivalent about the sacrifices that a serious onslaught on unemployment would require, it is, I believe, unrealistic to expect from politicians such exceptionally courageous leadership on these difficult issues. And only those who can honestly say, hand on heart, that they would not be tempted to switch their votes away from the party they currently support, if it took such steps as these in relation to taxes and pay, can fairly throw stones at the politicians who hesitate to take this kind of action in order to reduce unemployment.

I leave you with that thought.

4. Do the Unemployed Have the Answers?

Mike Allen

LISTENING TO THE current debate on unemployment is like going through, all over again, the painful months of losing my own job. Like so many people who became unemployed through the closure of their workplace, I have seen the disarray and confusion which come with economic failure on a small scale.

When the company I worked for in Galway got into trouble we were all brought together to try to save the jobs. Ideas were proposed and people got very hopeful and excited. But we had only started into the new approach when some other aspect of the crisis hit. We all came together again. Different ideas came forward and were accepted with renewed enthusiasm.

Six months – and six bright ideas – later, the situation had seriously deteriorated. At this stage, somebody suggested the first idea again, but this time it was rejected. 'It didn't work last time,' we said. The fact was, of course, that it had never been tried the first time – only proposed and agreed and then abandoned as things got worse. A sense of impossibility set in. Closure was inevitable and nothing in our control could stop it.

In Galway in 1985, I and a hundred others ended up on the dole, some of us for a long time. And now we are watching the same process at national level. Solutions are taken up from a never ending carousel, tried in a half-hearted fashion, then discarded in favour of the next idea that comes along.

Every week there is a barrage of proposals: tax cuts, interventionist job creation, an all-Ireland trading area, sectoral plans for forestry, fishing and food, Telesis, Culliton, linkage, structural funds.

Now, there is nothing wrong with any of these ideas. All have something to contribute, yet all are greeted now with cynicism by large numbers of Irish people because we have heard them so many times before.

Like a small business reeling in the face of economic crisis, Ireland has failed to make a consistent attempt to implement any of the useful and effective solutions which have been put forward.

During those months and the years that followed, I had a sense – which few people seemed to share – that it didn't need to be like this. Beyond all the individual and social damage that unemployment causes, its most corrosive effect must surely be its ability to convince us of its own inevitability. The Irish people have faced an unemployment problem so severe and so protracted that we have come to see it as a natural phenomenon. It is like the weather, you can complain about it or leave the country to get away from it, but you can't change it.

Yet, our high levels of unemployment are far from the norm in most developed countries. Our unemployment rate is over 16 per cent; the EC average is just over half that at 9.5 per cent, while even in the middle of a recession, Sweden and Japan keep well below a quarter of our level.

Our problem is too few jobs, not too many people. You can see this clearly when you look at the numbers in work instead of the numbers out of work. Austria is not exceptional in finding jobs for over 40 per cent of its population, we can only find jobs for 30 per cent of ours. That extra 10 per cent of the population in work would wipe out our unemployment.

When I used to hear on the radio that, say, Japan or the USA was lamenting its rising unemployment, it seemed to confirm that our situation was universal and intractable. Only after becoming involved in the unemployed centre and

looking at the figures myself did I realise that other Governments were worried about unemployment levels of less than
half our own, and would consider ours unthinkable.

One simple comparison demonstrates the scale of our
failure and yet how close solutions actually could be: if
Ireland had matched the percentage job creation achieved by
Spain in the 1987–90 period, we would have halved instead
of near doubled our level of unemployment.

Nothing in the economics columns of the papers convinced me that the time I wasted on the dole queues was inevitable. Only when I read a book called *Why some peoples
are more unemployed than others*[1] did I begin to see the deeper
cause behind the ever changing economic recipes. The book,
by Swedish writer Goran Therborn, looked at a number of
countries which have consistently achieved full employment
since the Second World War.

Therborn found that while such countries as Sweden,
Switzerland and Japan had very little in common in terms of
their economic system or natural resources, they shared two
essential features. Firstly, a national consensus that full employment is of overriding national importance, and secondly, the existence of institutions to carry this sense of priority
into action. Ireland has neither of these.

The result of this has been to consign one-fifth of our
potential workforce to a partial life, where potential is not
fulfilled, hopes are not realised and lives are stunted and
wasted.

While many people are sympathetic towards the unemployed, the impact of medium-to-long-term unemployment
can never be fully understood by someone who has not experienced it. Even listening to the experiences of others,
there always remains a part which says, 'That's not how I
would react, I would be different'.

In my own case, as a graduate returned from Britain
only a few years previously, I joined the dole queue confident that I would pick up a decent job. After several months
of working to re-open our old workplace as a workers' co-
op, trying my hand at a small service business and watching

equally qualified people begin to give up hope, I wasn't so sure.

When you first sign on, you quickly notice that there are two types of dole queue which assemble on different days: the unemployment benefit queue is made up of people whose payments are made as of right and have been in work relatively recently; the second and longer queue is for the people whose income is means-tested, who have either never worked or last worked so long ago that they have exhausted their social insurance payments. When you join the first queue, you notice that the other is full of people who shuffle, wear scruffy clothes and leave the exchange very quickly. Fifteen months later, when you graduate yourself to the second queue, you no longer notice these things, they have become part of your life.

In the seven years that I have been involved with unemployed organisations, most of what I have read describes this process as unemployed people 'losing confidence in their abilities', or 'suffering a decline in their sense of self worth'. The truth is that you have your confidence knocked out of you. It is not a passive slipping away due to lack of attention, it is an active, violent process of humiliation and hurt by society at large.

In those years, I have heard stories of casual humiliation and of struggles to retain dignity which far outstrip my own experiences, yet always renew me in the sense of anger and indignation I felt the first week I signed on. All of the stories revolve around the everyday features of legislation which mark the boundaries of the lives of the unemployed.

Unemployed people have to be 'Available For Work'. A member of an unemployed group in Co. Cork used to mow the lawn for his elderly neighbour while he had a job. After he became unemployed, he was questioned about this in the Exchange; they wanted to know if she was paying him. When he replied that she wasn't, he was told that he wasn't available for work while he was helping people out. After several weeks of threats to cut his dole, he stopped mowing her lawn. Now the elderly woman thinks that he – like the rest of the unemployed – is lazy.

Legal requirements, such as that to be 'Genuinely Seeking Work', appear reasonable even to sympathetic observers, but are oppressive to the people they affect. Exchanges regularly ask for a list of factories visited, adverts replied to, responses from prospective employers, and proof of registration with FÁS.

In fact, few people get jobs by cold calling at factory reception desks. Many industrial estates have signs up to discourage this form of job seeking which is inefficient and time-consuming for employers. Most employers don't reply to postal job applications. Most people in Ireland hear of jobs through personal contact. Around 90 per cent of job vacancies are filled by people already in work.

Few things can be more damaging to self-esteem than to offer yourself repeatedly for hire to employers who have no vacancies, and so face rejection after rejection. In many European countries – notably those with low levels of unemployment – all vacancies must be notified to the state recruitment agency. They can be filled in any suitable way, but people using the state recruitment offices must at least have a chance of applying. Here we have a system that requires unemployed people who are seeking jobs to seek them in FÁS, but does not require employers to offer them in FÁS. The vast majority don't.

Under our legislation, people are encouraged – no, *obliged* on penalty of losing their income – to carry on a job-seeking behaviour which we know is personally destructive and largely ineffective.

The cruel truth is that, even without threats, people who have been unemployed even for very many years continue to seek work. This doesn't mean that they apply for every job in the paper or cold call the local industrial estate every morning; it does mean that they are constantly on the look out for suitable work, and seek it out when they think they have a chance. Explaining this reasonable approach to the Exchange can lead to losing your income.

A further example of how the world looks different from

the dole is that of the schemes designed to 'Give Them Back Their Dignity'. A number of men who have now set up an unemployed group in the north-west were formerly employed on a social employment scheme there. Their employment was to cut hedges and, presumably to save money, they were given equipment from the 1930s with which to do it. In the months that they struggled with the old tools to cut a couple of miles of hedgerows, the full-time council worker, using modern equipment, cut every other hedgerow in the county. Leaving this pointless scheme would have meant losing their dole. They were left feeling angry and powerless, their time and effort totally unvalued. All of this was justified as 'Giving People Back Their Dignity'.

It is of course true that some people can receive the dole and help their neighbours, a few get jobs through cold calling at factories, and most schemes are not as destructive as the one I have described. From my experience, however, such events, small and large, make up the fabric of the lives of unemployed people.

When you have been unemployed for a long time, you develop strategies to survive. People develop rigorous time schedules or strange hobbies. They learn to survive on very low incomes and find ways of occupying their time. That doesn't mean that they are happier this way. A burning anger and a sense of injustice are liabilities if you have to survive years of unemployment. Every unemployed centre has been approached by pale men, clutching manuscripts in which they have transcribed the litany of injustice done to them. I have read too many of them: it is real injustice and, quite frankly, nobody cares.

These strategies for getting by collapse when people turn to look at their children. You can take it for yourself, but not for them. Everybody wants a good life for their children – and that includes a decent job.

In a Dublin school, two young girls, waiting with their class to visit the zoo, were put off the bus and sent home. Their parents – unemployed lone parents – had not paid their few pounds to the recreation fund. That day can never be recovered for those children, but what desperation for resources drives a teacher to such a cruel decision?

In a now famous remark quoted in the Tallaght Unemployed Centre's excellent *Our View At Last*,[2] an unemployed man said that his greatest fear was in a few years walking down to the Exchange with his son.

A man I interviewed about the Government's 'Jobsearch' course expressed the same transfer of hope and fear to his children. He said that the job-seeking skills in the course had been useful. 'Not for myself,' he said, 'but so I'll have something to pass on to my children.' He was forty-five.

Some theorists argue that mass unemployment is the beginning of the 'end of work', a new leisure society in which people no longer have to survive by the sweat of their brow. They say that the only issues are income and the right to do voluntary work. No unemployed person I have met agrees with this view. If there is to be less work around, surely we should divide it equally among us, rather than some choosing to have it all and others being forced to have none.

Many people casually say that we will never have full employment again. But if there is always to be unemployment, why does it always have to be the same people who suffer it most? Why should the child born in Ballymun be so much more at risk? Why the man from Tallaght? The woman from Moycross?

Irish society has become as blind to the injustice of unemployment as it is dazzled by its supposed inevitability. Part of the reason for this is the way in which we have divided our society so that those who are reasonably comfortable are not confronted with the injustice done to those who are not.

The largest concentrations of unemployed people live in the big public housing estates in our cities. This concentration is mostly caused by the housing policies of the 1970s and 1980s when employed people were given grants to buy houses elsewhere. They left behind them an ever increasing distillation of people without jobs. Such estates in Limerick, Dublin and Cork have unemployment rates – as measured by the local unemployed centres – of over 80 per cent.

When you walk through these estates you see a huge amount of maintenance work crying out to be done: grass in public areas uncut, park swings broken, pot holes in roads, community halls closed for long periods because of a shortage of caretakers. What sort of a society places people in an environment crying out for the enhancing effects of human labour and then tells them that there is no work?

These estates are a ferocious and personal insult to the people who live in them and they are an image of the type of Ireland we have built. Their opposite is found in the new middle class estates in south Dublin and elsewhere. These new groupings of brick townhouses curl up around themselves, their backs bristling with fence posts against the outside world. The only point of access is a high iron gate controlled 24 hours a day by a security guard.

This form of division, in which the unemployed and poor are seen primarily as a criminal threat by those who have possessions, is not a motor for progressive social change. In the absence of an understanding of what it is like to be unemployed and in the absence of a collective Irish vision of full employment, this is the inevitable reaction of those who are better off.

So, if we have failed to choose to build a full-employment Ireland, what do we do about it? If our employment culture is pro-property, anti-risk, anti-unemployed and anti-jobs, is that the end of the story? Are we back to where we started with the bland statement that unemployment is part of what we are?

People of all political persuasions and of none have told me that things are like they are because the unemployed are not organised and not effective enough in demanding their rights. I believe that this viewpoint is just a new way of saying that it is our own fault: 'If they don't protest, they must be doing nixers or getting enough on the dole'. Many historical explanations of poverty come down to saying that the poor are morally depraved; the failure of the unemployed to close ranks on the streets is just another sign of their moral depravity.

I have spent most of the years since losing my job in Galway in supporting unemployed organisations and arguing for the rights of the unemployed. Unemployed people face severe problems when they seek to develop as a mass pressure group.

Most organisations of marginalised people build solidarity and positive feelings around their identifying characteristic. 'Gay Pride' or 'Black is Beautiful' take the point of common identity – which was previously a focus for exclusion or shame – and transform it into a focus of pride and common solidarity. Women's rights or gay rights or travellers' rights organisations want to improve their status, not stop being women or gay or travellers.

'Proud To Be Unemployed' is a non-starter. Certainly, unemployed centres and action groups argue that there is no shame in being unemployed, but taking pride in a situation which is forced upon you is quite a different matter. Unemployed organisations are engaged in attempting to eliminate the feature which is their only common identity.

There are only certain experiences of unemployment which are likely to lead to the type of collective identification which would create an effective, popularly-based group.

Firstly, where large numbers of previously employed, unionised workers lose their jobs. Such workers have the fresh sense of outrage as well as the experience of organisation and strength. This was the case in Ireland in the 1950s when an effective lobby was built around redundant construction workers. The wave of redundancies in the 1980s did not create such a response, possibly because redundancy payments cushioned the initial impact. No wave of such newly unemployed activists is expected now.

The second experience of unemployment which could provide a basis for organising is very long-term unemployment. People in these circumstances are more willing to identify themselves as 'unemployed' and so can use it as a common bond. The isolation, lack of money and organisational experience and the well-founded cynicism of this group, however, create a major barrier to organisation.

Uniquely in Ireland returned young emigrants provide a third group of unemployed persons who can act as a potential basis for collective action. Such people, having worked abroad and learned that things are not inevitably the way they have always been, are impatient for change and unwilling simply to wait. I believe that this group offers perhaps the greatest hope for the development of a vision of Ireland which is better.

These reflections are offered in no spirit of apology. It should be clear by now that I don't believe that the responsibility for solving our unemployment crisis lies with the unemployed themselves.

Speaking to an audience of unemployed people who are thinking of setting up a group, of course, I emphasise the historic truth that nothing was won without a struggle, and that unless unemployed people demand their rights, nothing will be given to them. Such clarion calls are necessary in building our organisation and an organisation *is* being built. But talking to a wider audience it is necessary to ask – why is it that the unemployed must organise and march and demand before you ensure that a decent human life is available to everyone?

Such a question flies in the face of Ireland's recent claim to be a 'consensus society'. Affairs from wage agreements to European union were approached in a consensus manner. Yet unemployment has continued to rise and the consensus to deepen.

To many unemployed people and their organisations, this 'consensus' was simply an agreement to ignore our suffering. In the 'contented society' described by Professor John Kenneth Galbraith, the two-thirds who are getting on all right repeatedly vote down the change demanded by the remaining one-third who are suffering. In Ireland the two-thirds went further and claimed to be a 'national consensus'.

Only the trade union movement spoke up for the unemployed, winning only concessions when total change was
needed. Unemployed people and organisations were excluded from the consensus on exactly the same terms as we are
excluded from society.

How could we be part of a consensus which said that
the right approach was being taken when nothing got any
better for us and there were, day after day, even more of us.
In what way could we be invited to 'consent' to that?

Unemployment is now 80,000 higher than when I lost
my job. Sometimes I wonder if there is any hope of the type
of society that chooses full employment as its national goal.
If every consensus is designed to tell us everything's okay, is
the only way forward the years it will take to build an organisation strong enough to win our rights through conflict?
At other times, I know there is a vision of a better Ireland
that we can all subscribe to, a different type of consensus
which chooses a society with room for everyone. A consensus which unemployed people could be part of too.

For years unemployed organisations have argued that a
National Forum on Unemployment is the way forward.
Bringing unemployed people within the attempt to establish
a consensus would transform our ideas of how we run our
society. The greatest weakness of such an approach is that
the existing social partners hold their place because of the
economic power they wield. The unemployed hold no such
power, so simply being 'at the table' is not enough. A widely
held vision of an Ireland of full employment is needed to
give the necessary weight to the outsiders' voices.

Despite the blindness to the injustice of unemployment,
which I have pointed out, I believe that we in Ireland, due to
our size and history, have a real possibility of – and even
desire for – a sense of collective good.

To bring the unemployed into the consensus will hurt.
We can create more wealth and jobs, but if we cannot do it
fast enough, what there is will have to be shared around
more equally.

The unemployed and their organisations do not have all

the answers, nor should they be obliged to provide the impetus for change that our comfortable society needs. But without the unemployed inside the consensus, creating and participating in a vision of a better Ireland, there will be no answers for anyone.

Footnotes

[1] Goran Therborn, *Why some peoples are more unemployed than others: the strange paradox of growth and unemployment*, Verso, London, 1987.

[2] *Our View At Last. The OVAL Report*, Tallaght Centre for the Unemployed, Dublin, 1992.

5. A System that Cannot Deliver

Raymond Crotty

THE JOBS CRISIS is a new manifestation of an old problem. For 180 years, every second person born in Ireland has failed to get a livelihood here. The deprived half of the population, in the past, either starved to death or emigrated. Now they join the 300,000 on the dole queue.

Fewer people get a livelihood in Ireland now than at any time in the past 250 years, a period during which the world's population and its workforce have increased over sevenfold. The number of people at work in the Republic now is only one-third as many as 150 years ago. During the 70 years since the state's establishment, while the number at work here declined by 12 per cent, the number at work worldwide more than doubled; the number at work in Europe almost doubled; and in the UK it increased by 60 per cent.

Ireland's failure to provide a livelihood for its people for nearly two centuries is unique in human experience. Occasionally, the job losses have appeared to be arrested or even reversed; but invariably the abatement has been temporary. The jobs created by industrial protection in the 1930s disappeared as soon as protection was withdrawn. In the 1960s and 1970s, which was the age of 'the Irish economic miracle', 100,000, or 10 per cent, were added to the number of jobs in the country. But the job increase was more mirage than miracle and disappeared in the 1980s, when the exhaustion of the state's credit ended the public sector deficits that created the jobs. The reported increase in jobs since 1987 is due entirely to a change in the manner of counting jobs, and not in job numbers themselves.

WHILE THERE is nothing comparable in the western world to the Irish people's failure to get a livelihood, the Third World does offer parallels. The economies of the Third World, generally and over the long term, have performed less poorly than Ireland's; but their peoples, unlike Ireland's, have been unable to escape, by massive emigration, from the consequences of their seriously malfunctioning socio-economic systems. Their impoverished numbers swell in a vast morass of human misery similar to that which existed here in the mid-nineteenth century, before being relieved by famine and massive emigration. 'There, but for the emigration of every second person born here during the past 150 years, goes Ireland', might well be said of Somalia now.

It is at this level of generalisation that an explanation is to be sought and found for Ireland's jobs crisis. Ireland, and all those other 140 or so countries which are commonly referred to as the Third World and which contain over half of the world's population, share a unique experience. All of them, during the past 500 years, have been colonised by one or other of the nine countries which, with Greece, Luxembourg and Ireland, now comprise the EC. Those metropolitan countries, for profit, imposed their own individualist, capitalist institutions and technologies on colonised societies that were neither individualist nor capitalist. The abiding effect of that imposition is that, in every Third World country, there are now more people experiencing worse poverty than ever before; in Ireland, fewer people get a livelihood than at any time in the past 250 years.

Central to that imposition of cultures was the concept of property in land. Land which, in Ireland as throughout the non-European world, had been a resource available for the support, effectively or ineffectively, of the whole people, was made the property of the agents and collaborators of the colonial power, and of their heirs and assignees for ever. Land's purpose thereafter was to generate profit for its owners. The role of the people was to be the means of generating that profit according to changing market conditions.

Immediately after the Tudor conquest in the seventeenth century, the market was for cattle and sheep; and the people were driven 'to hell or Connaught', or carried off to work as slaves on West Indian plantations in order to leave the land clear for profitable livestock. Later, that market ended and was replaced, first by one for provisions to feed the slaves on the West Indian plantations; and later still by a demand for cereals, butter and bacon to feed England's industrial masses during the early industrial revolution. To cultivate the land in order to supply that market, with great profit to the proprietors of Ireland's land, Ireland's population was expanded rapidly, supported only by the exotic potato crop, which had recently been introduced from the highlands of South America. But then again the external market changed and cattle and sheep became once more profitable. The people, in response to this market change, were wiped out by famine and emigration, leaving the land clear once more for the now more profitable cattle and sheep.

Independence for Ireland, as for all other former capitalist colonies, has been largely a cosmetic affair: the flags, emblems, anthems, and the colour of the pillar boxes have been changed; but the fundamentals have not. Most fundamentally, the role of land has not changed. In order to increase land's profits now, within the EC, Ireland's consumers, including the 300,000 unemployed and their 600,000 dependants, must pay twice as much for their food as it can be bought for on world markets. Each Irish household pays, on average, £20 per week more for its food than is necessary. The benefits from this accrue to the less than 1 per cent of the population who account for 80 per cent of Irish farm output. In order to secure that profit for land, Irish industry has been exposed to worldwide competition, including competition from Korea, Hong Kong and Singapore, where workers buy their food at world prices.

Because the fundamental institutions and laws governing Irish society did not change with independence, the performance of that society has not changed either. The number getting a livelihood has declined in the 70 years since independence as it did in the preceding 70 years of colonial rule. Half of those born here have emigrated since independence as they did previously. True, thanks to emigration, living standards have risen since independence, but by no more than in the preceding 70 years.

Ireland, for 70 years of independence, has lived with institutions and fundamental laws imposed for metropolitan benefit, notwithstanding the unmitigated national disaster and degradation that these have caused for five centuries. It has done so because the casualties of Ireland's imposed, malfunctioning socio-economic system have not been around to press for change. Millions starved to death in the nineteenth century. Other millions have emigrated leaving a 'fat cat' society, for whom, mawkishly, 'Ireland is the best little country in the world'.

HOWEVER, FUNDAMENTAL change now appears imminent. This is because, while the institutional framework and the basic laws imposed on the nation by its colonial masters have not been changed, and, while the manner in which society as a result operates – especially in denying a livelihood to half of its members – has not changed, the people themselves have. They have been changed by an annual average 1.6 per cent rise in real incomes, secured through the emigration of every second person, throughout 140 years of colonialism and independence. The people now have real incomes that are eleven times greater than 140 years ago. Because of that, they are no longer willing to face the modern equivalent of the coffin ships of 140 years ago; nor to face existence on a British dole, which they did 60 years ago to escape from Ireland. The safety valve of emigration no longer works. The casualties of a fatally flawed socio-economic system accumulate in a jobs crisis, as they did in a morass of poverty 150 years ago, before famine and emigration relieved it. The jobs crisis, as it has developed over the past 20 years, creates pressures for change that did not exist when the casualties died quietly from famine or slipped away on the emigrant ships. An aspect of those pressures for change is that, in contrast to the remarkable stability of Irish politics in earlier years, every Government has been voted out of office in every general election since 1969.

The jobs crisis is compounded by the exhaustion of a series of expedients that has been available to successive Governments since independence. The promise of prudent, patriotic national government in the 1920s; the protection of the 1930s and 1940s; deficit financing in the following 40 years – each of these, in turn, seemed to offer hope; but are now all exhausted. There only remains their legacy of a massive state debt, the cost of servicing which, relative to GNP, is, like the country's unemployment rate, the highest in the world.

The state for decades, like a fairy godmother, injected into the economy borrowed purchasing power, over and above what it removed through taxation, that was annually equivalent to 6–7 per cent of GNP. There now has been a role reversal. Because of old debt and the exhaustion of credit, the state now, Scroogelike, must take out of the economy annually to pay interest on the debt far more than it can return in services and transfer payments. The politically balmy days of low taxes and large grants have been followed, as night follows day, by the stormy times of high taxes and meagre or no grants.

The chips are down. An ass-and-cart economy, which is the product of a colonial past and provides a livelihood for only half the people, with the end of emigration is now required to support all of the people. But the standards of the people are not ass-and-cart standards; they are the Henry Ford, if not the Porsche, standards of neighbouring peoples. None of these neighbouring peoples, from whom Ireland gets its standards, shares its colonised history. Most of them have benefited from their colonising pasts. Stripped of the expedients of the past, Ireland's political leaders are reduced to infantile exercises like the Culliton Report, which are comparable to fussily re-arranging the deck furniture while the *Lusitania* sinks. Various members of an economics establishment that has disgraced itself, morally and intellectually, by condoning for decades policies that were clearly headed for disaster, now peep above the parapet and sound off about the need to adjust down to ass-and-cart living standards.

However, after 140 years of sustained improvements in income made possible by emigration, the people are unlikely to accept any reversal towards the potatoes and skim milk days of our forebears – especially because of the ineffectualness of any such reversal. Holding down incomes would cause a classical brain-drain, as the best and brightest left to secure the better opportunities readily available for them abroad. Lower wages and lower corporate taxes would simply add to profits that are already large, and swell their outward flow. Together with foreign investment by Irish financial institutions, repatriated profits now remove from the economy £1 in every £4 produced by the Irish nation.

The confrontation implicit in Ireland's jobs crisis is without precedent. It is rooted in the inability of a socio-economic system imposed during a colonial past to cope with present needs. It is an inability that is shared by all of the 140 or so other former capitalist colonies which now comprise the Third World. The impotent poverty of the Third World's masses precludes confrontation there. The emigration of the disinherited half of the Irish has hitherto precluded confrontation here. But emigration has ceased and confrontation now rapidly mounts.

No former capitalist colony has broken the mould of perpetual socio-economic retrogression. All of them, like Ireland, retrogress. But because change is unprecedented, it is not necessarily impossible. People are not atoms, enslaved to immutable laws of conduct. Social institutions, made by people, can be changed by them also. But because fundamental change in the institutions and laws imposed by capitalist colonialism is unprecedented, its successful implementation can be guided only by first principles, not by precedent.

Two principles are particularly germane. First, as the crisis is an Irish national one, only the Irish nation can resolve it. Nowhere else has half the population for almost two centuries, failed to secure a livelihood; and while individuals may continue to resolve their individual problems by emigration, securing in Ireland livelihoods for all the Irish can be achieved only by collective, national action. Others will not – cannot – resolve this Irish national problem.

Second, given that, after 70 years of independence, half the Irish still cannot get a livelihood here; and given that the 140 or so other former capitalist colonies have likewise failed to develop, although some of these in the past had cultures far superior to that of contemporary Europe and some of them have been independent for a century longer than Ireland, it is evident that action, to be effective, must be radical. It must reach to the capitalist colonial roots of the problem. That is to say, successful resolution of the jobs crisis requires reform that is both radical and nationalist.

THE IMMEDIATE cause of the jobs crisis is Irish incomes and returns to labour which, as a result of the emigration of half the nation for almost 200 years, are determined by incomes and wages in the countries to which the Irish emigrate, not by economic conditions here. The latter only determine the proportion of the Irish who can secure a livelihood here at those externally determined incomes. That proportion has been about half the population for nearly 200 years.

The reason the economy can now offer jobs to only half the population is in part because of past emigration. This has kept the population small and the economy correspondingly unproductive. The larger populations and faster economic growth in the countries to which the Irish emigrate have enabled those countries to attain the scale of production necessary for their high incomes – high incomes to which the Irish aspire but which a small, unproductive economy can only provide for half its people.

Greatly exacerbating the problem of externally determined incomes that are beyond the capacity of a small, unproductive economy to deliver is a great wedge of costs inserted between what Irish workers get and what the final user of labour pays for it. That wedge of costs on labour, relative to what the suppliers receive for their labour, is greater in Ireland than in any other country.

The wedge is built up in a number of ways. The unnecessarily high food costs resulting from the EC's Common Agricultural Policy is one way. Because Irish people spend about twice as large a proportion of their low incomes on food as the people of other EC countries, unnecessarily high food costs raise their living costs more, and reduce their competitiveness here.

Property is hardly taxed at all and profits are taxed very lightly in Ireland. Public revenue, therefore, is derived disproportionately from taxes on labour. Of that public revenue, which comes mainly from labour, either directly through PAYE and PRSI or indirectly via VAT, a much higher proportion than in other countries is pre-empted to pay interest on the state debt, an expenditure from which Irish workers receive no benefit.

The jobs crisis feeds upon itself. With an unemployment rate that is more than twice as high as in the rest of the EC, more taxes than elsewhere must be levied – mainly on labour – to finance unemployment benefits and assistance. Again these higher taxes mean higher labour costs and, therefore, less employment and more unemployment.

Unemployment benefits and assistance, that are higher relative to lower wages here than they are elsewhere, also contribute to the jobs crisis. Because these payments are withdrawn if unemployed people earn money, they are effectively a 100 per cent tax on the putative incomes of the unemployed. Because they are paid only if people remain idle, they are, as well as being a tax on employment, a subsidy to unemployment.

A SOLUTION to the jobs crisis is to be sought by minimising the cost of labour to its users, including those who use only their own labour. That can be done by transferring public costs that now fall on labour to the nation's land and savings where, on grounds of equity and economic expediency, these public costs should lie. This would involve the imposition of appropriate revenue-maximising taxes, the elimination of inappropriate public expenditures, and the allocation of the funds thus realised as a national dividend, payable to every resident citizen on the voters' register.

A revenue-maximising tax on urban and rural land would yield several billion pounds annually, of which a good deal more than half would probably come from urban land. Indications of the potential revenue from this source are the £9.4 million recently paid for a four-and-a-half acre site in the Dublin suburb of Ballsbridge; or the £100 annual rent which farmers regularly pay for an acre of farmland; or the 25p which they pay to rent a gallon of the nation's annual EC milk quota of a billion gallons.

The Irish banking system is one of the world's most successful. It secured its success at the nation's cost. The banking system did this for over a century, by acting, in the words of the state's first Minister for Finance, 'largely as a conduit pipe for the taking of money out of the country for employment outside'. The system more recently has profited even more by expanding the money supply to make capital cheap while simultaneously, through inflation, making labour dear. This laid the foundations for all the great fortunes of modern Ireland, which have been acquired simply by replacing labour made dear by policy with capital made cheap by policy. Most recently, the Irish banking system, with associated financial institutions, has been profiting by again transferring the nation's savings abroad. Revenue-maximising taxes on the assets of the banks, in conjunction with an appropriate exchange-rate policy, would secure for public purposes very substantial revenues while simultaneously terminating the Irish banking system's disastrous capacity to profit at the nation's cost.

Many Irish taxpayers were old enough to vote recently only for the first time. Many are still too young to vote. Yet all will be required in 1993 to pay over £2 billion in taxes to service a debt created by politicians few of whom the tax-payers knew and even fewer of whom they ever voted for. The debt was incurred by the politicians allegedly to create jobs; but there are now many fewer jobs than before the debt was created. This is because the debt creation was, in fact, part of the process of making capital cheap for the privileged, through grants, subsidies and tax holidays, by making labour dear through the taxes now required to service the politicians' debt.

This country has reached the stage where servicing a debt incurred by irresponsible rulers is no longer practicable. The country should recognise this and do as virtually every country in the world has done in similar circumstances at some stage in its history. That is, effectively to cease to pay interest on the debt.

The revenue secured from taxing the nation's land and banking system, together with the public expenditure saved by ceasing to pay interest on the state debt would be sufficient to pay an annual national dividend of £3,000 to every one of the 2.6 million citizens on the voters' register. That dividend would be receivable by right of citizenship and residence in Ireland.

Social welfare payments, including unemployment benefit/assistance, which are now made to relieve destitution, would no longer be needed by citizens in receipt of a national dividend and could, therefore, be terminated. Unemployment would be eliminated, at least in the important sense that no citizen would be required, as 300,000 now are, to prove that they had performed no socially useful service as the condition for receiving the pittance on which they and their dependants now survive. The number at work would increase, partly because the suggested reforms, while raising the real incomes of workers through a national dividend, would simultaneously reduce the cost of labour to its users, through the elimination, or reduction, of existing taxes on labour; and partly because persons who are now unemployed would no longer be taxed at 100 per cent of earnings through the withdrawal of unemployment benefit/

assistance. That increase in the number at work, through scale economies, would raise total output more than proportionately and so average output would also rise for all workers, including those now with jobs. Whether or not everyone chose to work would be immaterial. All would have the choice to do so, which the combination of unemployment benefit/assistance, PAYE and PRSI now denies to half of the Irish labour supply.

THE PROPOSED reforms, or others designed to deal with the crisis caused by the half of the population which previously emigrated no longer doing so, if successfully implemented, would have consequences extending far beyond Ireland. For, in making it possible for all the Irish to get a livelihood in Ireland, the reforms would meet the Third World's greatest need, which is for the precedent of a former capitalist colony escaping from the hitherto invariable mould of socio-economic retrogression which capitalist colonialism imposes. That Third World need for a precedent, if met, would promise to end the great problem and scandal of a swelling mass of poverty and degradation in a world where the technology and resources exist to end physical want worldwide.

6. A Strategy for Full Employment

Peter Cassells

*When the factories are all closing
like they are in our home town
and your friends are looking out for work
that's nowhere to be found,
When the spirits they need a risin'
to be happy, proud and strong,
It's time to sing, it's time to sing
to sing a powerful song.*[1]

THESE FEW LINES, written by Davy Carton and Leo Moran of the Saw Doctors, capture much of the spirit of what I want to say about the jobs crisis. The sentiments, delivered in an assertive tone and with a slight hint of stridency, convey the non-defeatist and positive attitude we need in confronting this crisis. It is indeed time for us to sing a powerful song – a song that no longer confines responsibility for job creation to those who sit around the cabinet table or in the boardroom, but channels the creative energy of all our people towards this task.

I AM not going to repeat the litany of gloom, the unemployment statistics that are bandied about at the end of each month but which don't always convey the realities behind the figures. Instead I would like to take a couple of minutes to talk about the importance of having a job by telling you about a man we'll call Seán.

On my way to Athlone last month, I gave Seán a lift. He is 31 years of age, married with two young children, one at primary school and the other due to start next September. He was one of those people who are great company when you're driving – ask one question and you get a detailed and colourful two or three minute reply.

Seán's father had emigrated back in the late 1940s. But he returned in the early 1950s in response to Bord na Móna's recruiting campaign – offering work on piece rates of 2/1 an hour and living accommodation for 20s. a week.

Seán is one of three boys and four girls reared on a labourer's wage that was hard earned on the boglands around Clara. He belongs to the first generation of his family to benefit from free post-primary education. He worked hard at school and in June 1980 he got, to quote himself, 'a good Leaving Cert with a few honours'. In the 13 years since he sat his Leaving Cert exam, Seán has *never* had a steady job or a decent well-paid job.

In his own words, he's had 'bits of jobs all right'. He got some summer work with Bord na Móna when times were good, he worked as a driver with a farm contractor cutting silage for a few months, he did stable work on a Kildare stud farm and drove a private bus at weekends. His wife got the odd few hours hotel work for weddings and dinner dances.

Seán does not want to emigrate – he has worked 'off and on' on building sites in England but, as he says, 'It's hard to get a start there now with the slump on the buildings'. He has strong local ties and wants to stay there. '*One decent factory,*' he told me, '*would make all the difference.*'

Meanwhile he is living from day to day hoping that something will crop up. He plays football with the local team and plays with a group that gets a bit of work at functions – 'If it wasn't for the bit of crack,' he said, 'there's times I think I'd go mad.'

Seán's story is repeated the length and breadth of Ireland – in every townland, village, town and city. It is not just rural communities that are threatened by unemployment. Many working class communities in our cities have had their hearts torn out by the scourge of unemployment. There are whole streets in Dublin, Cork, Galway and Limerick where no one has a regular job.

THE SCALE of this problem and the failure of high levels of economic growth to translate into a large number of jobs, has led some people to conclude that people like Seán will never work again – that high levels of unemployment will always be with us – that we somehow have moved into a post-industrial leisure society and should accept but re-define unemployment. I believe that we should reject this conclusion.

In the longer term, broader definitions and a deeper understanding of the creative content and productive value of all work may blur the rigid distinctions between employment and unemployment as we know them now. But this is no consolation for the women and men who are today ex-cluded from active involvement in the Irish economy. At the moment, a job gives us a wage packet and a decent wage gives us access to a decent life. Work also fulfils many of our needs – it gives us dignity, a social value, a chance to make our mark, to do things, to be somebody. So we can't make unemployment go away by simply redefining it.

Others believe that it will go away automatically if there is a return to strong economic growth not only in Ireland, but in Europe and the United States. I don't think so. Strong economic growth is needed. But the relationship between economic growth and employment has changed with changes in technology and the structure of production. Growth on its own won't create jobs. Also, half of the unem-ployed are now out of work for three or four years and will not be drawn back into employment as a result of economic growth without special measures.

There is also a small group of people who believe that, as a country, we cannot do better than our current achieve-ments and that demographic change – a fall off in the num-ber of school-leavers – will solve our unemployment prob-lem in the year 2000. I am sure that, like me, the reader finds this approach equally unacceptable.

No! Unemployment will not go away of its own accord. We ourselves must face up to the daunting challenges before us. Each and every one of these daunting challenges is a consequence of the long-term failure to develop the Irish economy in line with the economies of other European countries. I believe that, within the lifetime of the current generation, we can achieve low levels of unemployment and higher living standards. Not by the introduction of more make-work schemes, but by changes in industrial policy, radical tax reform and new and radical thinking in the following key areas.

NEW INNOVATIVE thinking is what Ireland needs most at the moment. There is a growing recognition that innovation has become a critical factor in determining the survival and prosperity of organisations, companies and countries. However, while the awareness of the importance of innovation is growing, we tend to see the important and real innovations as being technological or structural and often do not realise the critical importance of innovation in thinking. Whether an organisation, company or country flourishes or declines is as much dependent on the quality and relevance of the thinking underlying its strategies as on the machines or resources it possesses.

New thinking on the basic assumptions underlying our strategies is not easy and we tend to avoid it. Changing beliefs does not come easy to any of us individually or collectively. Technological and even structural change is much easier. However, in an era of rapid and fundamental economic and social change, such as we are now in, it is vital that we ensure that the assumptions underlying our strategies for developing the economy and tackling unemployment are relevant to the emerging reality.

As John Maynard Keynes pointed out, 'politicians can be prisoners unknowingly of some obsolete economists', and can waste resources on strategies which are focused on confirming and recreating the past rather than on designing, nurturing and being a guide for the future. Keynes himself demonstrated in the 1930s, through his initiative in rethinking some economic assumptions, that the wealth-creating capacity of a society can be dramatically altered by a slight shift in thinking. At the moment, Ireland badly needs innovation in thinking. Otherwise, we risk becoming prisoners of a number of obsolete economists.

For a start, we should recognise that the nature of political economy is changing rapidly throughout the world. Hard-line policies and ideologies of the new right and the old left are no longer relevant or credible. Apart from Mrs Thatcher herself, there are few Thatcherite hard-line free-marketeers left in Britain, and in America the Reagan-Bush school of unfettered free-market economics closed down this January. There are now so few advocates of state-controlled centralised economic planning left that they can hold their AGM in a Lada.

In the European Community, most Governments now accept the *social market* as the fairest and most effective way of combining market economics and social equity. While here at home our tiny band of New Right economists have deserted the snug in Doheny and Nesbitt's in favour of the richer pastures of the stockbroker's office and a slice of the action on the currency markets.

This time of weakening extremes is an opportunity for strengthening consensus on economic strategy – a time for drawing on the best of the free-market tradition and the best of the interventionist tradition. The time is now ripe in Ireland for a radical new departure in our approach to formulating economic policy. This is particularly urgent in relation to our policies for tackling unemployment and creating jobs.

๑ The Irish Congress of Trade Unions has proposed that all the elected parties in the new Dáil should agree to form a Political Consensus for Jobs. The new Dáil should put together a four-year strategy for protecting existing jobs and creating new jobs. Out of the consensus for jobs would come a *Programme for Jobs* which would provide a blueprint for action over the next four years. ๑

The Political Consensus would also agree on the broad outlines of a longer term economic strategy to develop Ireland over the next decade as a modern, efficient social-market economy similar to Germany and other advanced European countries. Representative social and economic organisations should have an input into the formulation of these strategies through the proposed National Economic and Social Forum provided for in the Fianna Fáil–Labour Programme for Government.

I believe that this new Political Consensus for Jobs should be informed and energised by the following principles:

* A recognition in this country that the right to work is a fundamental human right and that providing every citizen with the opportunity to exercise that right is a primary aim of economic policy.

* Acceptance of the need to create an economic environment, which will encourage enterprising initiatives by individuals, companies, co-operatives and communities and that we need entrepreneurs as much as we need dockers and dentists.

* Also an acceptance of the need for selective state intervention when key players in the free market are unnecessarily threatening existing jobs or ignoring profitable opportunities to create new jobs.

* We should also recognise that increased productivity from a highly-skilled workforce using modern technologies is the most effective way of generating wealth and improving our standard of living. We need a clear understanding that the fruits of this high productivity economy will be shared by all citizens in a manner that reflects our political commitment to social equity and a better quality of life for all our people.

This proposal for a Political Consensus for Jobs is not a

proposal for an all-party Government, nor is it envisaged that political parties would forget about their economic policy differences. It is a case for a new way of doing an important part of our political business and is intended to reduce political conflict in one area where political differences often have more to do with form than content. The proposal is based on two very obvious facts of political life in this country

1. No party has a monopoly of economic wisdom or social concern.

2. The differences between parties on economic policies and strategies are not so fundamental that common ground cannot be found on an agreed strategy for tackling the jobs crisis.

TACKLING THE jobs crisis will also require more than innovative thinking at the political level. Our success in creating jobs will depend on our ability to produce goods and services that the people of Europe need, of a quality that they require and at prices they can afford. To do this we need capital, materials and workers, but the key element that makes it all come together and produce jobs is enterprise and entrepreneurship.

In Ireland, we urgently need new thinking on what we mean by enterprise and entrepreneurs.

Two of the most striking things about entrepreneurs in Ireland is how few of them there are and how limited they are in what they do. Our first crop of industrialists was incubated behind the secure walls of tariff protection. With a guaranteed market on their doorstep they failed to expand their horizons beyond three or four green fields, created few jobs, and many of them did not survive the opening up of free trade in the 1960s.

Those entrepreneurs who were willing to think big and take risks, especially with their own money, were few and far between. Apart from the economic environment, the social attitudes and values in Ireland were not conducive to producing high-powered, innovative entrepreneurs capable of developing massive companies with thousands of jobs. Indeed, such people were not only commercially envied but spiritually suspect ... we all learned that it was more difficult for a camel to pass through the eye of a needle.

The real folk heroes were perceived to be the small-scale entrepreneurs, most of whom had inherited their businesses and created few jobs. Merchants and traders of all kinds, building contractors, quarry owners and publicans were figures of respect and gratitude. That many of them did not believe in paying decent wages or taxes was overlooked by those who believed that a stained-glass window in the new church was more than adequate compensation for such minor worldly misdemeanours. Those who worked for them have a very different story to tell from Alice Taylor's wistful tales in *Quench the Lamp*.[2] The playwright Tom Murphy got much closer to the bone of material hardship, psychological subordination and social tyranny in his play, *A Crucial Week in the Life of a Grocer's Assistant*.[3]

A step above this level were the nearest thing to real entrepreneurs – millers and bakery owners, bacon curers and farm machinery makers – many of them Protestant and therefore suspected of being Freemasons. Even in the capital city its industrial base was confined largely to booze and biscuits until the next stage in our economic development, the opening up of the country to international capital in the 1960s.

This change allowed a new crop of Irish entrepreneurs to piggy-back their way to prosperity on a package of incentives designed to encourage foreign investors to put their money into industrial projects in Ireland. Not only did they do this successfully and profitably, but for many years they did it so quietly that many people believed that only foreigners were eligible for state handouts.

The list of incentives, handouts and back ups, funded by the taxpayer, that was put in place is extensive and impressive. But they failed to bring us full employment. Too many of our budding entrepreneurs were more interested in creative accounting than creative capitalism. Their notion of the market seems to be confined to the area covered by their local chamber of commerce, and their marketing strategy a matter of deals made over a few drinks after the Rotary Club lunch. The potential for developing our natural resources was lost through sentimental but reactionary notions that farmers were the backbone of the country and farming more a way of life than an industry.

All of this must change. We need an entrepreneurial revolution in this country. We will have to stop thinking of business people as confined to those who were born with a silver spoon in their mouth or those who went from rags to riches by suspect means. Unfortunately, in Ireland too many of our business people fall into these categories.

The public rightly perceives the formula for business success in this country as a combination of pulling strokes, greasing palms, knowing the right people and playing safe at all times. This may not tally with the economic textbooks' definition of business acumen, but it is close to what you will be told anywhere more than two citizens are gathered to discuss the affairs of state. The dozen or so Irish companies who have broken out of this small-minded mould have shown what can be done.

To improve the quality and expand the quantity of our entrepreneurs we will have to widen the base we draw on to find entrepreneurial talent. Enterprise is not confined to 1 or 2 per cent of the population. It exists within the creative spirit of every human being in every community, albeit in differing degrees.

If we are to develop the numbers of large-scale indigenous companies in both the private and public sectors, which development the Culliton Report pointed out is an essential prerequisite for more jobs, we can only do this with the full and complete involvement of the people who work in these companies.

We should learn from those countries in Europe which have already achieved full employment. One of those lessons is that progress is not achieved through confrontation or rugged individualism, but through partnership and an approach to enterprise that releases the creative energy of all our people. I am talking about real involvement and real partnership along the lines practised in Germany – the most successful economy in Europe, if not the world.

THE THIRD area where we require new thinking is in the type of companies and businesses we wish to develop in this country. It would be a serious error to allow ourselves to be pressurised by obsolete economists into low-wage options as a means of tackling the jobs crisis.

 All of the evidence shows that such an option would fail to solve the problem of mass unemployment and would undermine the economic progress made in recent decades. Our future lies in a highly innovative, high quality, high skilled, high wage, high productivity society.

The classical economic thinking that low wages bring increased employment due to competitive advantage is obsolete. This concept refers to an economy in which unskilled labour was a major cost factor in production, and price was the primary determinant of competitiveness. Neither of these situations applies any longer in Ireland or in the European economy generally.

In the European economy, of which Ireland is now an integral part, unskilled labour no longer forms a significant part of the costs of production. Employment which requires large inputs of unskilled labour has virtually disappeared as it is automated or shifted to Asia. To attract it back would require us to impoverish ourselves by getting wages to lower levels than Shanghai where workers are paid £200 a year: even if this were possible, the value of this kind of work is questionable.

The new jobs now emerging in Europe are knowledge-intensive, not labour-intensive. In this type of production process, which depends on a high level of skill and technology, low wages do not automatically mean lower labour costs. In fact, the reverse is the reality; low wages tend to go hand in hand with lower productivity and high unit labour costs.

If we look at the European economy we see that it is the highest wage countries which have the lowest unemployment, while low-waged countries like Ireland have the highest unemployment.

Another reason why the idea that low wages give comparative advantage is obsolete is the fact that in the affluent knowledge-based economies of today, innovation, quality, uniqueness are as important or more important than price. Any company or organisation wishing to grow and generate new employment requires the invention of new services or products or new forms of marketing, a continuous stream of innovation.

Achieving this goal will require people with high skills, motivation and creativity. In a low-wage economy these people will quite simply not be available – a policy of low wages in a developed economy like Ireland is a recipe for low skills, low standards of living and a high rate of unemployment.

Developing this type of company in Ireland will also require a change in our approach to the introduction of new technologies. Technologies should be used to support people not to replace people. What is often not realised, and I know this from my trips to Japan and from discussions with companies and unions there, is that the Japanese success in raising productivity and generating employment came about not primarily because of advances in technology, but from innovations in 'human resource management' – the empowering of the workforce through shop floor team-based working.

World Class Manufacturing and Total Quality Management are Japanese concepts that Irish companies will have to adopt if we are to create more jobs. These systems are based on recognising the essential role of workers in improving the quality of the goods and services provided by a company. The companies of the future must embrace social partnership and secure the involvement of their workers through co-operation and consensus.

These companies of the future must also see their goal as the maintenance and creation of employment. Grants, tax breaks and wage agreements should all be tied to a 'jobs audit' where each company has a clear investment programme for generating new products and new employment. The idea that good management results in shedding jobs must be seen as anti-social and essentially a reflection of a failure in management strategically to think out and invest in creating the future.

IN CONCLUSION, I believe that these three radical changes in our thinking, along with investment in bold imaginative projects on the same scale as those that turned our rivers and bogs into electricity and the shamrock into a symbol of international travel, with changes in industrial policy, tax and PRSI reform, and the expansion of skilled training programmes, would go a long way towards tackling the jobs crisis.

The resources of every citizen in this country, their energy and their goodwill must be inspired by the target of wiping out the blight of unemployment. The scale of the task facing us demands the kind of political courage and foresight which has transformed other societies. It also demands that we have the widest agreement possible on strategies to maintain and create jobs. Such agreement will require compromises from all of us. Let us hope that we have the courage to make them.

Footnotes
[1] 'Sing a Powerful Song' (D. Carton/L. Moran) from the album *If this is Rock 'n Roll I Want My Old Job Back*, The Saw Doctors, Solid Records (Ire), 1991.
[2] Alice Taylor, *Quench The Lamp*, Brandon Book Publishers, Dingle, Co. Kerry, 1990.
[3] Thomas Murphy, *A Crucial Week in the Life of a Grocer's Assistant*, Gallery Press, Dublin, 1978.

7. The Regional Dimension

Gearóid Ó Tuathaigh

WITH OVER 300,000 people unemployed in the Republic of
Ireland, the declared priority of all political leaders (indeed
of all community leaders) is the maintenance and creation of
jobs. This is so even among those who recognise that the
very concept of a 'job', as it has been understood traditionally in modern society, is undergoing radical interrogation.
The economic cost of this waste of human resources is enormous, the social cost perhaps incalculable. It is little wonder
that 'putting the country back to work' has become the
political slogan of the hour. But, so pressing is the acknowledged need to create viable employment for Irish people
that one is entitled to ask, does it matter whether the jobs are
in Crossmolina, Cork or Crumlin? Indeed, one may go further and ask whether, in the light of our ardent embrace of
the Single Market in the EC, the matter of *where* Irish people
find jobs within the single European labour market is any
longer an issue of any consequence. Labour mobility is un-
questionably part of the logic of a single, integrated and
dynamic labour market. In this context, there are those who
would contend that any talk of 'creating jobs in Ireland' (and
a fortiori, in any particular parts of Ireland) is misplaced and
out of date, the product of obsolete thinking. If we accept the
logic of a single labour market, there is a case for saying that
the geographical distribution of employment should not –
indeed must not – intrude upon the primary task of generating employment in a dynamic economy for all those seeking

employment throughout the European Community.

Does it matter, therefore, where Irish people find jobs within the single European Community labour market (to say nothing of the wider labour markets to which the Irish have traditionally gravitated and to which they still have limited access, in the USA and the old British dominions)? Well, it certainly does seem to matter to large numbers of people, not least to those political leaders charged with formulating development policy at an EC level and in Ireland itself. From its very inception, in the Preamble to the Treaty of Rome, there was a commitment among EC leaders to strengthen the unity of the economies of their states and regions, and to ensure their harmonious development by reducing differences in living standards existing between the various regions. Various policy instruments were devised for achieving these objectives of 'balanced regional growth and development', or convergence, as it came increasingly to be called. These policy instruments initially included the agricultural funds (notably the Guidance Section), the European Social Fund (ESF) and the European Investment Bank. The terms and the operation of these underwent numerous amendments in response to changing circumstances and an ongoing evaluation of their effectiveness.

After the first enlargement in 1972 (with the accession of the UK, Denmark and Ireland to the Community) the debate on regional disparities became more urgent and, in many ways, more challenging. A specific instrument of Community regional policy was created in 1975, with the establishment of the European Regional Development Fund (ERDF), and in the past decade or so, following the accession of the Mediterranean countries (Greece in 1981, Spain and Portugal in 1986), there has been a series of reforms of these various structural funds. Not only have they been increased in size, but the underlying objective of virtually all the changes of the past decade has been to achieve a higher level of integration between the various measures proposed in regional development programmes, a shift away from individual projects towards integrated programmes in the proposals eligible for support. When the Single European Act set in motion the steps for the creation of a single market, the commitment to regional 'convergence' was re-affirmed (and indeed fortified by the explicit mention of the regional funds instrument in the Act) in the following terms: 'The creation, therefore, of an integrated market and a technological community needs to be supplemented by a very substantial effort to strengthen the Community's cohesion by promoting regional development and the convergence of living standards' so that 'the Community shall aim at reducing disparities between the various regions and the backwardness of the least favoured regions'.

The major increase in the structural funds and the establishment of the special cohesion funds at the recent summits, taken in conjunction with the efforts of the Commission to secure a sharper focus on priority regions and a real degree of integration in the structural funds supports, are indications that it is appreciated that more comprehensive and substantial interventions will be needed on the part of Community agencies and policy instruments if there is to be any measurable progress towards the goal of convergence or balanced regional growth and living standards throughout the regions of the Community. More significant, perhaps, than the specific policy instruments charged with a direct role in regional policy, is the evidence in recent debates of the growing acceptance at all levels of the Community's power-systems that all Community policies have implications for inter-regional convergence or divergence. The differential impact on different regions of *all* EC policies is now accepted, and the logic of the Single Market, in terms such as labour and capital flows and the distribution/concentration of services, is being faced with a little more candour even by the most ardent European 'integrationists'. In sum, it is possible that all policies will in future be interrogated from the perspective of their inter-regional impact rather more systematically than has been the case to date.

At a national level here in Ireland we have also given explicit recognition to the concept of a regional policy since the early 1950s (though nationalist rhetoric had preached the gospel of highly dispersed economic development long before the establishment of the State). Numerous instruments of regional policy have been designed during the past 40 years: the establishment of Designated Areas in the twelve western counties, with higher levels of manufacturing aid; the setting up of the Shannon Free Airport Development Company (SFADCO), and of Gaeltarra Éireann (later, in altered form, Údarás na Gaeltachta) with a regional development remit; the establishment of Regional Development Organisations and of County Development Teams, and, perhaps most significantly, the regional structure and responsibilities of the IDA (with, at one time, region-specific job creation targets, in the interests of 'balanced regional development') and of Bord Fáilte. More recently, the process of consultation for drawing up proposals for inclusion in the national plan for EC structural funds involved a number of regional advisory groups. While, finally, in late 1992 the Government announced the establishment of County Enterprise Partnership Boards with limited development responsibilities.

It is clear, then, that at EC and at national level there is a strong consensus among policy-makers (no doubt reflecting a consensus among their electorates) that it *does* matter where people live and work, that the objective of 'balanced regional development' is a sound political objective. We may ask, in passing: why does it matter? On what grounds is the concept of 'regional balance' advocated? The economic arguments for balanced regional growth in job creation generally rest on considerations of equity and efficiency. The 'efficiency' argument includes, among other issues, the proposition that the most efficient use of resources is that which mobilises the total resources of the entire extent of any geographical area (this, incidentally, begs the question as to why the mobilisation of the human resources has to be *in situ*). There are other aspects also to the efficiency argument, notably the issues of social costs and other disutilities arising from excessive urbanisation.

An interesting new emphasis in recent EC documentation on the future of rural society (in the aftermath of the Common Agricultural Policy reforms) is the proposed justification for maintaining rural settlement on the grounds that rural society performs a vital custodial function for a balanced environment:

> But our rural areas are not only places where people live and work, for at the same time they have vital functions for society as a whole. As a buffer area and refuge for recreation, the countryside is vital to the general ecological equilibrium, and it is assuming an increasingly important role as the most popular location for relaxation and leisure.[1]

The sceptic may see in this rhetoric an attempt to rationalise the need for reduced production in European agriculture (in the interests of sustaining prices) in terms which valorise the virtues of an eco-sensitive rural economy.

However, it may well be that, ultimately, it is in deep social and cultural impulses that we must seek explanations for why it seems to matter greatly where people have jobs and lead their lives, by their own choice. A deep-seated sense of place; an attachment to ancestral home and place; a desire of parents to have their children settled near them; a desire on the part of many people to remain in an area where they feel culturally anchored, where they feel a depth of association and can enjoy an accretion of memories and associations which confirm them in their sense of identity in space and time: these are some of the factors at work. Of course, this will not apply with equal force to everybody. The imperatives of personal ambition may require a break with family and locality; upward social mobility may require outward physical mobility in the form of migration or emigration. But the social reasons – at an individual and collective level – which rest on continuity of settlement, a sense of rootedness and belonging, and the desire for social reproduction in a named human habitat, are all deep human instincts which must be admitted in any explanation of the importance attached to the desirability of a geographical spread and 'balance' in economic activity and employment opportunity.

If the EC and national political institutions have adopted balanced regional growth and the elimination of regional disparities among their objectives, and have devised policy instruments to achieve these objectives, we are entitled to ask: how successful have these policy instruments been? In the context of the European Community we must conclude that the policies have not succeeded in bringing about inter-regional convergence in living standards throughout the Community. Some of the reasons for this failure are easily listed. The specific instruments of regional policy – the various structural funds – were inadequate in size and inadequate in their geographical concentration. There was for long a poor understanding of how the specific regional programmes might be compatible or in conflict with general economic and social policies being pursued by the EC or by national governments. Clearly, the structural funds were too small to counter the tendency of some major Community policies actually to exacerbate regional disparities. (This was so in the case of the product price-support aspect of the CAP, which actually worsened inequalities between the commercially developed and the peripheral agricultural zones within the EC and, indeed, within Ireland itself).

So far as Irish regional initiatives are concerned, while it is true that regional disparities have not been corrected during the past 20 years, it is important that we attend to the complexity of the evidence. Throughout the 1970s the IDA succeeded in meeting industrial job-creating targets in several of the most disadvantaged of its nine regions (for example, the West, the Midlands, the North-west). With net in-migration in Ireland in the 1970s, many rural areas experienced a stabilisation or increase in population, largely due to the growth of certain towns in many counties. At the same time, however, Dublin did not benefit from this regional industrial policy, losing almost 40,000 net industrial jobs during the 1970s and 1980s. The Dublin region's share of national industrial employment, as Drudy's work has shown, fell from over 37 per cent in 1971 to 27 per cent in 1989.[2] But Dublin's service-sector employment grew throughout these years (though at a slower rate during the 1980s), and its share of national population grew also. Furthermore, while industrial job creation had some successes in many regions in the 1970s, the overall situation was not so encouraging: the increase in industrial employment could not compensate for loss of employment elsewhere in the rural economy (notably in agriculture), so that *total* employment growth in the rural areas was below the national average even during the 'buoyant' 1970s. Moreover, studies have identified short-comings in the industrial strategy itself; in many instances it encouraged the use of capital more than labour; it over-relied on migrant branch factories of transnational com-panies, often with low linkage to the indigenous sector or with high 'leakage' of profit, investment or even of con-sumer spending out of the local economy. In the difficult 1980s, of course, job losses became more punishing in all regions, and the creation of new jobs has consistently failed to keep pace with the combined total of those entering the labour market for the first time and those who have lost jobs and are seeking new employment.

Regional disparities persist. Emigration rates in the 1980s had a differential impact on different regions, and per capita income in, for example, the North-west and Midlands still lags significantly behind the national average. The diffi-cult 1980s have, of course, seen real problems and real pov-erty in every region, and regional averages mask many local variations. While the rural crisis of unemployment leading to migration and emigration is starkly revealed in the tearful parting at regional airports after the Christmas holiday at home, or in the complaint of local GAA clubs that they have difficulty fielding teams at various grades, the impact of un-employment in the large urban centres has produced its own harrowing landscape of social deprivation. In general terms, however, it is clear that regional disparities within Ireland have not disappeared in either good times or bad during the past 30 years.

IF THE regional policies pursued to date have had only limited success, then what are the prospects for balanced regional development in job maintenance and job creation under the conditions in which we find ourselves and those likely to prevail in the immediate future, including the published programme of the incoming Government? Whatever context we adopt for answering these questions, the prospects are full of uncertainty and contradictory signals.

In global and European terms, much depends on the lifting of the recessionary gloom, the establishment of stability and order in currency markets, and on a general quickening in economic activity and world trade. Some areas allow for firmer forecasts. In post-CAP European agriculture, it is clear that the era of product price supports and expanding production is over; much agricultural land will cease traditional food production and the number of farmers intensively working their land for a living will decline significantly over the next decade.

These changes will affect Ireland in many ways, but especially in the development of Irish rural society. EC rural development programmes will stress agri-tourism and more extensive diversification of economic activity in the rural areas (through the creation of clusters of dynamic SMEs – small- and medium-size enterprises – based on indigenous resources and a commitment to innovation); the development of alternative land uses with a strong environmental awareness and conservation bias in the forms of land use will be favoured in Community support measures. This diversification and SME development strategy will be hard-pressed to take up the shake-out from the contracting labour force in farming. (For example, the increased significance of knowledge-based enterprise is recognised by governments in all developed countries – gaining competitive advantage in this highly competitive market will not be easy, as the state of the computer industry testifies).

It is fair to assume that population maintenance in many communities throughout rural Ireland (and especially in the most disadvantaged areas) will require various forms of income support in the coming decade.

HOWEVER, IN terms of generating dynamic economic and social activity based on the application of a policy of cohesion and balanced regional growth, the evidence suggests that, while the size of EC structural and cohesion funds may increase, they will remain small relative to total income generated within the Community; that an increasing portion of these funds will go to the southern (and, in time, perhaps the eastern) regions of Europe; that, while more closely focused on priority areas, the national government in Ireland will remain in the driving seat in determining how they are spent. In sum, it is unlikely that the structural funds *in themselves* will have a decisive influence on the differential impact of general EC policies across the regions of the Community (the completion of the internal market, developments in monetary union and other institutional reforms).

The structural funds will be useful and valuable to us in Ireland, particularly in funding our capital programme, but they are unlikely seriously to counter the logic of the internal market in, for example, enhancing the attractions of the developed core at the further expense of the periphery. If the declared Community objectives of cohesion and convergence are to be anything more than declarations, then the commitment to correcting regional disparities must permeate and be given due prominence in every area of Community policy (general budgetary policy, technology transfer, infrastructural investment, research and development strategy). In present circumstances it is difficult to avoid the conclusion that, notwithstanding the understandable satisfaction in Ireland at the announcement of the terms of the Edinburgh summit (with the promise of about £8 billion in structural and cohesion funds over 7 years), the structural funds in themselves are unlikely to close the gap significantly (in terms of productivity or GDP per capita) between Ireland as a whole and the EC average. Nor is it likely that the operation of other EC policies will rectify these disparities.

The structural funds will in the years ahead – as in the past – ensure that, whether it be infrastructural or industrial or social investment, we will not be as badly off as we would otherwise be without the structural funds. But, in the light of past experience and the relatively small size of the funds, they are not likely to bring about convergence in living standards between the existing regions of the EC (even without further enlargement). What impact these and other funds may have on inter-regional disparities *within* Ireland will depend on how our own Government at national level attends to the regional dimension of national policies in general, and to its specific uses of the EC structural funds in the interests of a version of 'cohesion' within Ireland. Here also we are faced with contradictory signals.

The Department of Finance will, it seems, continue to be decisive in determining the allocation within the state of EC structural funds. The changes in Irish agriculture (already mentioned) and their implications for the entire rural economy and society; the high volume of young adults who will continue to come onto the labour market for some time to come as a result of our demographic profile; the urgent need for measures directed at the enclaves of chronic unemployment and social demoralisation in Dublin and our other main cities – these and other factors will call for new economic activity and job creation on a scale which we have never so far been able to achieve. Irish industrial policy, now marching to Culliton's drum, will, it seems, be directed in future more towards developing indigenous resources of every kind and at forming clusters of competitive enterprises thereon.

This suggested domestic context, even if generally sound, will no doubt seem somewhat abstract to the school-leavers, parents or community leaders of communities ravaged by emigration and unemployment, whether in rural Mayo or urban Moyross, in Darndale or Dingle, as they ask the basic questions: are there going to be jobs here for our children? What are the chances of our sons and daughters being able to get a viable job in their own area when they

leave school? What chance is there of mature men and wom-
en who may lose their jobs in middle age – or for whom
subsistence or small-scale farming ceases to be a viable
source of income – getting jobs in the city centre, in the suburbs or in country towns or villages throughout Ireland? The
regional dimension of employment refers, after all, to all regions, including Dublin. The fact that we have an exceptionally centralised state by European standards, or that a disproportionately high percentage of the total population of
the state is concentrated in the greater Dublin area, has not
saved Dublin from having to endure exceptionally heavy job
losses in manufacturing employment during the past 20
years, so that it now suffers from some of the worst unemployment black-spots in the country (with all the attendant
social problems).

Given all the circumstances, it is likely that in the short-
to medium-term some towns and villages will lose more jobs
and will be further bled by the haemorrhage of emigration.
The loss of population and of key institutions (school or post
office) may further loosen the social bonds and damage the
morale of more rural communities, leaving them lingering
on in a sad state of social anaemia. There may be more
towns hit hard by the loss of its major employer through the
closure of a factory, without even the solace of the Saw Doctors to give voice to their anger or to prompt their community to fight back. The problems of structural unemployment
in certain urban or suburban enclaves of our major cities
may prove depressingly resistant to the efforts at corrective
state intervention.

On the other hand, there are numerous signs of communities taking steps to mobilise themselves in the interests of
their own development, indeed survival. In the west of Ireland, the call by the bishops on communities to fight for
their survival has, on the evidence to date, struck a strong
chord; promising local development initiatives have emerged under the EC Leader Programme; inner-city groups have
begun to harness community effort and resources in the task
of community renewal and revival; the recently announced

Government Programme contains many proposals which, if implemented, could offer real nourishment to these seeds of enterprise and development. It may indeed be likely that unemployment will rise in the short term, during 1993, and that there will be a large pool of 'jobless' people in rural as well as urban Ireland for some time to come. But, if the failures are to be limited and the seeds of recovery properly rooted, then we must take time to consider fundamentals. Specifically, if a national policy of economic recovery and job creation is to be infused with a genuine concern for balanced regional development, then we must address some basic questions. These questions will remain even if the currency and interest rate crises prove temporary, the international economy shows signs of recovery, and the Government's employment strategy begins to have significant and enduring impact. One of these basic questions, to which I now turn in the final part of this lecture, is the question of institutional or structural reform.

THE PRECISE configuration of political and administrative institutions most likely to achieve an acceptable (and demonstrably beneficial) balance between local empowerment and national state or EC resource re-allocation will need careful attention. The debate on subsidiarity – what ought to be left to local or regional bodies, and how power and resources and responsibilities should best be integrated into democratic structures – is a complex one; one fears that while experts differ, communities may continue to wither. But there is unlikely to be too much argument against the conclusion that the exceptionally centralised Irish state has not succeeded in achieving an acceptable 'regional balance' in economic chances or living standards.

The various instruments of national regional policy have had some degree of success within their own terms of reference. This is true of the regional dimension of the IDA industrial jobs/projects strategy in particular (and of SFADCO and, in its job-creation role, of Údarás na Gaeltachta). It is more difficult to evaluate the specific contribution of the

regional tourism structure to general inter-regional development. But these different instruments of regional policy have
not been part of an overall integrated policy framework. The
IDA no doubt responds conscientiously to its obligations
(and to the urgings of its political masters at national as well
as local level) to secure wide dispersal in its job-creation
efforts; no doubt it has to evaluate the social as well as the
physical infrastructure likely to determine decisions to locate
factories or businesses of any kind. But it must take these
'infrastructural' resources pretty well as it finds them.

The decisions on the location of educational facilities,
roads, post offices, leisure facilities, to say nothing of banks
or theatres – all facilities relevant to the chances of a town or
a village being able to create the social milieu likely to make
the young want to stay and the entrepreneurs want to invest
and settle – must be taken as part of a coherent appraisal of
the basic needs and the real prospects of communities, rural
or urban. For example, if we take a basic community in rural
Ireland as a parish or village of about 2,000 core population,
with a church, school, post office, petrol pumps, shop and
pub as basic institutions of community, who is to decide
which of these will live and which will wither and die? Will
it be the closure of the post office or of the school that will
herald the death knell, or are such closures more the result
than the cause of terminal decline? Or, if we take a town
(with anything from about 2,000 to 10,000 population, and a
catchment area of about 10 miles radius), we can list essential services in the economic and social infrastructure as
schools (first and second level), post office, church, banks,
supermarket, health-care centre, Garda station, leisure facilities – hotel, cinema, dance-hall, pool-hall, sports fields – and
some manufacturing units. The closure of a factory – especially if it is a significant employer – is not merely an immediate economic reversal for such a town, it is also a severe
psychological blow to community morale. It is likely to
precipitate out-migration and to trigger off a circular and
cumulative process of decline and enfeeblement. In the depressed inner-city areas of high unemployment and severe

social problems we can identify a distinctive, but comparable, process of cumulative disadvantage and community impoverishment.

What should an employment policy seek to do in these circumstances – the circumstances which, in one way or another, account for our 300,000 unemployed? The IDA (or its successor *Forfhás*) can be encouraged, indeed instructed, to strive for regional balance in industrial job creation (with regional offices to facilitate this); Bord Fáilte can be instructed to do likewise; from time to time sections of the central bureaucracy can be packed off to different country towns; priority consideration can be given to specific unemployment black-spots in the major cities. But is it realistic to expect that every village in the country can or will prosper; that the IDA or SFADCO can ensure a viable factory or cluster of SMEs in every town? Would it not be more honest to admit that there will have to be choices; that, when all factors are weighed, some places will prosper while others won't, that there will be winners as well as losers, determined by the results of competition and the rewards of local leadership and enterprise, as between one town and another? Is not this natural and inevitable, and should we not accept it as such, instead of denouncing it in terms of the cruel Darwinian logic of market forces?

This line of argument is, in fact, seriously flawed. The fate of towns and villages and inner-city neighbourhoods – whether they wax or wane as communities – is not simply determined by the invisible hand of market forces. It is also profoundly affected by innumerable decisions and choices made across the broad spectrum of public policy. It is in this context that the case for institutional change becomes relevant. What is lacking at the present time in Ireland is an appropriate and immediately responsible framework of political and administrative institutions at sub-national level, where integrated development of regions or local communities, involving choices and decisions, can be reconciled with the essentially democratic ideal of responsible local government taking as much responsibility as possible for the development of its own community. Of course, the division of powers, responsibilities and resources between regional or local bodies and the national state (or the Community institutions) will have to be argued about and negotiated. But a start must be made.

It is possible that a start was intended with the County Enterprise Partnership Boards announced in late 1992, though there were signs that this particular proposal had been brought forward with too much haste: the non-elective character of the proposed boards, the limited finance, and certain terms of reference (notably relating to tourism) will all need reconsideration. But, at the very least, they seemed to be an acknowledgement of public disquiet at local level at the apparent powerlessness of local communities in the face of excessive centralisation in decision-making.

More recently, the Programme for Government announced in January by the new Fianna Fáil–Labour coalition has in it certain commitments to structural reform which may prove to be important. Specifically, the programme re-affirms the decision to establish the County Enterprise Boards and also restates the commitment to a regionally balanced employment strategy for the revamped IDA. But it also promises 'to accelerate the progress of local government reform and the devolution of funding from central government to local authorities so as to give greater scope for local initiative in decision making'. It also explicitly promises that:

> New regional authorities will be established in 1993; elected members will be given additional reserved powers, the devolution of additional functions to local authorities, covering the areas of competence of several departments, will be progressively implemented in the light of the recommendations of the Barrington Report.

The precise terms of these proposed reforms in regional and local government will be awaited with interest. In particular, it is important that it be delineated clearly how the new structures will relate to the regional employment remit of the re-vamped IDA (*Forbairt*) and other development agencies, and also how meaningful a role they will have in respect of the decisions on resource allocations from the structural and cohesion funds over the next 7 years. If one is inclined to temper enthusiasm with caution in these matters, it is only a sensible attitude, in the light of our past experience of baulking at serious structural reforms.

The fact that for EC purposes Ireland is considered as *one* region (a Government decision, the correctness of which was endorsed in the influential 1989 NESC report on Ireland's performance in the EC), has effectively meant that the power of the central state apparatus of government (notably the Department of Finance) has been overwhelming in determining the use of structural funds, and that, accordingly, several priorities within the overall Exchequer needs are likely to have prevailed over specifically regional criteria in the allocation of these funds. The sub-regional advisory committees set up in seven regions to co-ordinate submissions for EC support under the first phase (1989–93) of the new structural funds national plan (and more recently involved in co-ordinating submissions for inclusion in the phase two plan) seem, on the evidence to date, to have been a relatively weak advisory filter, and may, in fact, have added to the feelings of frustration and scepticism among local political and community leaders at their being involved in a show of regional participation which utterly failed to mask the unmistakable reality of central government's control of the agenda, the priorities and the allocation of EC structural funds.

Only time will tell whether or not the reforms proposed by the new Government will make a real difference to this system of heavily centralised decision-making. There is ample evidence that at European Community level there is a strong desire to see more effective participation at sub-national institutional level in the formulation and implementation of Community regional policies. Indeed, it is probable that the Commission would wish to play a more active and robustly interventionist role itself in determining the use of structural funds in the interests of integrated regional development. But in the current political climate, in particular British sensitivity at the prospect of any enhancement of the role of the Commission, it is unlikely that the Commission will be able to do more than exhort and, through occasional gestures (for example, facilitating direct access to token EC supports for sub-national groups, such as the western bishops achieved during 1992), to put pressure on the Irish Government to show greater urgency in addressing the particular needs of sub-regions *within* Ireland.

This is not to suggest that the mere establishment of genuine regional authorities, or general sub-national institutional reform, would be a panacea for all the problems of regional disparities. But, if it be true that power without responsibility is a danger to democracy, then it may be suggested that responsibility without power or resources is the embodiment of political absurdity.

OUR FAILURE to date to produce coherent policies for integrated regional development has been both conceptual and structural. We have not been notably creative in designing effective models of political 'subsidiarity' or regional 'cohesion' within our own state. A combination of a regionally-oriented industrial employment strategy and limited bureaucratic dispersal has not in the past provided 'balanced regional development', in terms of population, jobs, or living standards. This is in no way to denigrate the real benefits which the IDA, SFADCO or Údarás na Gaeltachta job strategies and the limited degree of administrative decentralisation have brought to towns and districts in various parts of the country. It is clear that 'balanced regional growth' in job maintenance and job creation will require a more sustained and comprehensive effort at devising and implementing integrated regional development strategies than we have managed to do so far.

'Integrated regional development' is not, it must be emphasised, a specific or set formula for achieving economic growth and social progress; it is not a discrete set of measures which, if implemented, would automatically guarantee certain results. In fact, 'integrated regional development' is best understood as a controlling idea through which to plan and to evaluate the inter-relatedness and the multiple implications of *both* market forces *and* the full range of public policies. In economic terms, integrated regional development is not, so to speak, high-tech surgery, but rather holistic health promotion. By the same token, the regional dimension is not simply that which concerns every place outside of Dublin: integrated regional development in Ireland must include the particular circumstances and needs of the greater Dublin area.

Accepting, therefore, that a concern with cultural transmission and with social continuity in one's own place is a deep-seated instinct in human society, we must recognise that in Ireland it does matter to most parents where their sons or daughters find jobs and settle down, and that it matters to many of those sons and daughters that they at least have the opportunity of finding viable jobs within the general area in which they have grown up and to which they have strong attachments of family and of sentiment.

In facing the enormous challenge of meeting the jobs crisis which afflicts Ireland today – and which seems set to continue to challenge us for the remainder of this decade – we as a people must give proper consideration to the 'regional dimension' of the crisis, that is, to the geographical distribution of economic activity and employment opportunity. The policies adopted for generating employment – whatever they may be – will inevitably have implications for regional balance. The manner in which jobs are created, and the kinds of jobs which are created are both linked, in a variety of ways, with *where* they are created. It behoves political and community leaders, therefore, to take due cognisance of this dimension in the formulation and implementation of public policy in every domain of economic and social life.

Nobody is demanding geographically frozen systems of social reproduction. Nobody is arguing for a renunciation or a curtailment of the individual's right to mobility (individual choice being a core value of the open society). But, in the dynamics of mobility, change and development which will move Europe into the next century, the ideal of 'balance' must be constantly interrogated and must permeate all our discussion of the public policies which are so important in determining our 'private' or individual choices. In short, in economic liberty's dialogue with the public good, the idea of 'balanced regional growth' is one of the key ideas which will test the rigour and ingenuity of our thinking, and the stamina and constancy of purpose with which we set about trying to shape our economic growth and social development in accordance with deep democratic impulses and with a proper respect for the deeply human sense of affection for and attachment to one's own native place and community.

Footnotes

[1] 'The Future of Rural Society', Community Communication to Parliament and the Council, *Bulletin of the European Communities, Supplement 4/88*, Luxembourg, 1988.

[2] P.J. Drudy, 'Demographic and Economic Change in Dublin in Recent Decades', in Andrew MacLaran (ed.) *Dublin in Crisis*, Trinity Papers in Geography no. 5, Department of Geography, Trinity College, Dublin, 1991.

8. The Semi-State Sector and Job Creation

J.J. Lee

THE PUBLIC SECTOR has played in Ireland, as in all advanced European countries, a major role, directly and indirectly, in economic development. Perhaps contrary to an impression sometimes given, nevertheless, we do not rely exceptionally heavily on public enterprise. We are about average by western European standards. It may be, however, that the idea of average does not make much sense. If there were a greater need for public enterprise here compared with most other western European countries, or indeed if there were less need, then being average could in no way be taken to justify the current position. We cannot derive comfort from averages. We have to analyse our own position from scratch.

This is easier said than done. How do we evaluate the performance of the public sector? In this country the instinctive criterion historically has been to compare ourselves with Britain in virtually every area of activity. But this may not be very helpful in this case. For one thing, the size of the British market is vastly greater than that of the Irish market, and much of the performance of companies, whether public or private, depends on the size of markets. We might even begin by asking whether there is a semi-state sector at all. Should we even be thinking in these terms? The only common feature of the semi-state sector is state participation one way or another. Unless it can be shown that this is *the* key factor influencing the performance of all the companies involved, then this way of looking at the question may blur rather than clarify the real issues involved. There is, after all, huge variety within this sector.

What, for instance, have Bord na Móna and the Great Southern Hotels in common? What have An Post and Coillte Teo, The Forestry Board, in common? Some companies, like Aer Lingus, face intense international competition. Some do not. It may be analytically far more illuminating to think in terms of the traded sector in the economy compared with the sheltered sector than to think in terms of public and private.

It is, of course, fashionable to draw the public/private distinction. The ideology of privatisation, associated in particular with Mrs Thatcher, seeks to capture the commanding heights of analytical activity by attributing economic performance to the source of ownership. This is a very nineteenth-century way of looking at things, regurgitating the arguments, or rather the doctrines, of capitalists and socialists and seeking to rejuvenate them for the late twentieth century. There may indeed be validity on one side or the other in these doctrinal disputes, although a historian accustomed to evaluating issues on the basis of evidence rather than dogma will be inclined to wonder if any economic doctrine can cover all circumstances at all times. The first question to be asked, therefore, about any public enterprise, is whether, and how, the nature of ownership affects its performance. That is a question that has to be asked, not an answer that can be assumed.

There can be little doubt that in some cases the answer to the first part of the question is 'yes'. But which cases? The quality of performance varies greatly within the state sector – just as it varies greatly within the private sector. Indeed, it varies greatly within individual companies over time, even when the nature of their ownership remains unchanged. It can be taken almost as a fact of nature that a monopoly (a private monopoly no less than a public one) will try to exploit the consumer. The main question here is: how can monopoly be most effectively controlled?

This is not an easy question to answer in practice. A bit of competition provides a great incentive for all of us. Too much competition can descend into chaos. The real question, from a national viewpoint, and particularly in a small country, concerns the optimum level of competition.

I mention a small country deliberately, because the fundamental problem confronting all Irish firms, public and private, is the minuscule size of the home market. The problems of many of our public-sector firms begin, not with their management or with their workers or even with the Government, but with the size and distribution of Irish population. No other country has managed its affairs, or had its affairs managed for it, over the last 150 years, in a manner which resulted in so bizarre a population experience. We talk a lot about how we compare with EC averages these days. One EC average we ought to keep firmly in mind for comparative purposes is population density. If we had the EC average, we would have a population of about 12 million. Of course, we can throw up our hands in horror and say that would be a disaster. We can't find employment for a population of 3.5 million in this part of the island. Another 9 million would surely swamp us. Maybe it would. I am not here suggesting we could cope with it, either in economic or in environmental terms. But we must also observe that others do cope. Indeed, the population density of Northern Ireland is double that of the Republic. If we had down here the population density of the North, we would now have a population of about 7 million in this state.

This has immediate implications for many of our state companies. Many of the best known operate in areas of activity dependent on the size of the market. The economies of scale that allow cheaper unit costs in supplying a big market than a small one apply with particular force in many of the public utility areas serviced by state companies like the ESB, Iarnród Éireann, Bus Éireann, Telecom Éireann or An Post. Remember the furore raised last year at the proposal to close down a substantial number of rural post offices. That proposal would not have been made if we had a normal population structure. Much the same consideration probably applies to the Shannon stopover dispute.

Controversies of this type serve to highlight fundamental issues. The management of the companies involved approach the questions from the point of view of the financial health of their companies. The communities affected approach them from a quite different angle – the health of the communities. Both are absolutely legitimate from their own point of view. The wider question that arises is: where does the national interest lie in situations like these? We have, unfortunately, done little thinking on the real meaning of the national interest. We scarcely have a framework of thinking about it, however ritualistically we invoke the rhetoric of national interest, particularly at election time. We consequently often get rather low-quality debates on the issues involved. The financial commentators seem to be confident of the correct answers, and Governments then scurry around, accused of making 'political' decisions, as sinners against the light of financial orthodoxy, rather than presenting their case – if they have a case – from a positive perspective.

We pride ourselves, to some extent rightly, on our pragmatism. But there are at least two types of pragmatism. Pragmatism can be an alternative to dogma in economic matters. In this case it is often devoutly to be welcomed. But pragmatism can also be an alternative to planning, however loosely defined. We simply cannot afford, in my view, not to plan in this country, in however general a sense. We have to have a sense of direction or we will consistently get the worst of all worlds.

That becomes particularly clear the moment we try to mobilise the state sector for job creation. The semi-state companies have, to some extent, always been seen as jobcreators. But the constraints are far greater now than ever before, just when the challenge is becoming more intensive. In earlier decades, when we were not so exposed to international competition, some state companies could adopt a relaxed attitude towards overmanning, confident that their political masters would understand perfectly. In fact, some managers may have come under intense pressure to take on more workers than they felt they really needed. The idea of reducing the size of the workforce, much less of closing plants, or liquidating entire companies, was not part of the intellectual culture of the state sector.

That changed in the 1980s. It will change even more in the 1990s. A cold wind has blown through the state sector, as through indigenous Irish industry in general. The number of semi-state jobs fell by about a quarter between 1980 and 1989, from 88,000 to 67,000.[1] As companies have to compete increasingly in a wider variety of areas, they cannot indulge in overmanning to any serious extent in the future. The Single European Act, by intensifying competition within the EC, opens wider opportunities for Irish firms to compete on European markets. But it also opens opportunities for European firms to compete on Irish markets. Several state-sponsored bodies could be vulnerable to pressure from, or even takeover by, much bigger foreign firms.

The ethos of the state company as providing secure pensionable employment for life is, therefore, likely to have to change in those cases where it has not already changed. The only choice is whether the change is voluntary and anticipatory, or involuntary and reactive.

The commercial state companies face a further dilemma. They are generally too small to compete internationally unless they expand, and expand significantly. They cannot expand very much in Ireland unless they diversify into other activities. But diversification brings its own problems. There is a widespread business view that one should confine oneself to activities closely linked to one's area of core expertise. Many firms in the private sector that have diversified outside their original areas of activity have registered spectacular failures, however glittering the parental track record. There is, therefore, a strong tendency for firms in small countries, like CRH or Smurfit, to expand abroad in their normal areas of activity, rather than diversify into unrelated activities at home, where they may be lacking management expertise.

Expansion, whether at home or abroad, means that one must be in for the long haul. The problems in TEAM Aer Lingus serve as a poignant reminder of that. This is one of the most imaginative, courageous and enterprising initiatives taken by any company in the country, public or private. We badly need initiatives like this to succeed, to provide high-quality employment for highly trained personnel, and to deepen our awareness of, and receptivity to, technological change. I am not sufficiently familiar with the details of the current difficulties to pass any confident verdict on them. But the fortunes of an enterprise like this ought not to be dictated by immediate short-term considerations. Short-term problems, if they are short-term, ought not to be dealt with in a purely ad hoc manner, but to be seen as an integral, indeed inevitable, part of longer-term development in a cyclical industry. That, in turn, means that if the state intends to back ventures of this type, it must find ways of ensuring that the company has sufficient capital, and that state-sponsored companies are not capital-starved at crucial junctures. Government must, therefore, be able to factor at least the broad outlines of these capital demands into its own forward financial planning.

One may argue that these companies should not expand, that the risks are simply too great. But the risks of not expanding are arguably even greater. The state sector contains a disproportionate number of the largest companies in the country. They may still be small by international standards, but they are the biggest we've got. And we have to rely on our largest companies to capture export markets for us, as well as, of course, defend the home market.

Big companies are normally the most successful on export markets. We do hear, it is true, a great deal about the success of small firms, particularly in the United States. We should obviously strive to create as many small firms as possible. But three things must be kept in mind when we invoke the American experience. Firstly, small in America is defined differently from small in Ireland. Many of the firms considered small by Americans are large by our standards. We must be certain that we are comparing like with like. Secondly, the vast bulk of American small firms do not export. They sell only on the home market, or even on local markets. They do not have to acquire the capacity to penetrate markets in different countries with different cultures and different languages. We will have to do that if we are to increase our market share in continental Europe. Thirdly, many small firms, whether in America or elsewhere, rely on large firms for their markets. They flourish as suppliers to larger firms, on subcontracting jobs and the like. One might almost say that the quickest way to build up a thriving small-firm sector is to develop a thriving large-firm sector.

The vast bulk of propaganda about job creation in the indigenous sector in Ireland today concentrates on the image of the self-starter, on this product of a new 'enterprise culture', of the rugged individualist trained to trample all before him, or her, in the ceaseless struggle for profit.

It is an engaging self-image in the age of the yuppie. But our main problem in job creation in this country is not, in fact, a shortage of small firms, or even of self-starters, however desirable it may be that we have more of them. The real challenge is not to found small firms. It is to grow small firms into medium-sized ones, medium into large, and what we now call large into really large, by international standards. The biggest single difference between Ireland and more prosperous smaller economies is not a relative shortage of small firms here. It is that virtually all these economies have a substantial number of really large firms, often several times the size of our biggest firms, including our state firms.

We, therefore, urgently need a strategy for large-firm expansion. This has to include the relevant firms in the public sector, even though, if it were to transpire that they might be more successful as private firms, or in some form of joint venture, then that option should be kept actively in mind. The jobs crisis is so serious, and the price inflicted on many of the unemployed so dreadful, that ideological disputes should be suspended until the back of the problem can be broken. The only ideology the jobs crisis should allow us to indulge is the ideology of excellence. The Culliton Report has some sensible things to say in this regard, and its recommendations should be implemented.[2]

There seems to be relatively little co-ordination of policy in the public sector at present. The semi-state companies report to different departments and different ministers. Their relations with their departments are governed by a host of conflicting considerations. The responsible officials in the relevant departments may or may not have had an opportunity of acquiring the degree of knowledge and understanding requisite for informed comment on company policy. The more companies become international, presumably the less will officials be qualified to monitor them. The boards of the companies are bound to vary considerably in quality, even where political considerations do not seriously influence the choice of members. The amount of business talent available in the country for overseeing the affairs of large firms, many of them in high-technology areas and, one hopes, many increasingly involved in international activity, is distinctly limited.

The wider problem of the state's approach towards the jobs crisis concerns the quality of the official mind. Nobody should dispute the high intelligence and dedication of many individual public servants. But it continues to remain astonishing, at least to me, what little attempt the state makes to mobilise the best minds in the country in the face of a crisis situation. When Peter Sutherland suggested recently that we were not nearly as dependent on the British market as we believed ourselves to be, because our trade with Britain really only came to between 15 and 20 per cent of our total foreign trade, as distinct from the 30 or more per cent we have widely assumed, he raised a major question about the quality of our analysis. It is amazing that an observation of such potentially fundamental importance, whatever responses it may elicit, should be left to be made by a private individual, however gifted.

We are often told – not only by civil servants, but by

businessmen and journalists as well – that we have plenty of
thought in this country, perhaps even too much thought,
and our real problem is lack of action. According to this
view, we have all the ideas we need. All that is missing is
the political will to implement them. But do we have too
many ideas and too little action? How many ideas is too
many? Might it be that those who take that view simply be-
tray an innocence of the supply side in ideas in the modern
world?

And in what way do we have too little action? We have
innumerable business-promotion schemes. The IDA is re-
garded as a formidable competitor among industrial development agencies around the world. The Culliton Report recommended drastic changes in a number of areas, including
FÁS. I am not competent to judge the recommendation. But
FÁS was itself the result of organisational changes introduced only five years before. If fault there was, it was not
due to lack of action, but to badly considered action. That is
a distinguishing feature of state policy in too many economic areas. There is no lack of action. But it is mindless action, ad hoc action responding in an incoherent manner to
perceived short-term problems. The incoherence is not acci-
dental. It is the result of intellectual incoherence. We do not
know how to think strategically, however repeatedly we
now use the word 'strategy'.

I am well aware that politicians have, for the most part,
no time to think beyond the immediate present. But we have
not even given ourselves the mechanisms for thinking strategically about industrial policy. The state does not even
think strategically about industrial policy in the semi-state
sector. Dr Michael Dargan, drawing on his extensive experience in both the public and the private sectors, recommended seven years ago 'a systematic examination' of the role and
performance of the semi-state sector. He recommended too
the establishment of 'a small council of persons of outstanding attainment, mostly from business' which should 'maintain contact with all the commercial state-sponsored bodies',
and which might at least serve to provide the overview so

sadly missing in our highly centralised but highly fragment-ed governmental structure.[3] It has not happened.

Part of our problem arises from our preference for rely-ing on gut instinct in place of the no doubt tedious, but usu-ally essential, evaluation of evidence. I praised the Culliton Report earlier. It is a courageous and challenging report. But it can also be criticised in terms of its use of evidence. It makes nearly sixty major recommendations. But these are not, for the most part, based on evidence within the Report. They are based much more on assertions than on evidence. It is, therefore, very difficult actually to engage in reasoned discussion about its conclusions. Many are probably right. But which ones? Consider its treatment of taxation policy.

Culliton concludes that 'in no other single area does the Government have at its disposal the tools to make as far-reaching and effective a reform to support an enterprise economy as in taxation'.[4] Many of us would probably agree with this. I would like to think that most of their recom-mendations are right. But when we turn to the back-up con-sultants' report commissioned by Culliton and presented by the eminent accountancy firm, Arthur Andersen, we find that the consultants are highly sceptical about the potential impact of taxation policy. They reject many of the claims regularly repeated by columnists and commentators. In many respects the Culliton Report simply ignores, and thus implicitly rejects, the consultants' views. Maybe the Report is right and the consultants wrong. But it would inspire more confidence in Culliton if it spelled out its evidence. The point at issue is not even in the first instance who is right and who is wrong. The point is that it is simply impossible to conduct an informed discussion of the impact of taxation, or anything else, on job-creation policy when assertions are presented as conclusions. There must be a better way of evaluating evidence.

Ireland has plenty of talented individuals. We have the ability to devise, and to implement, strategies for growth. But only the state can harness the intellectual ability, much of it now frittered away in a badly organised higher education system, to plot a path to the future, as well as provide the political will to focus on job creation as the prime purpose of economic activity. We still have not thought adequately about a strategy of job creation over the next 20 years. We devote only a derisory proportion of total public expenditure to systematic thinking about the use we make of that expenditure. It is now time to think in terms of a constructive and sustained partnership between the private and public sectors in ways that we have never considered before. It can be done. But we need to blend together in a creative combination the requisite will, intelligence, imagination and enterprise in what would be, for us, a pioneering approach. That is the challenge for the 1990s and beyond.

Footnotes

[1] Paul Sweeney, *The Politics of Public Enterprise and Privatisation*, Tomar, Dublin, 1990, p.45.

[2] *A Time for Change: Industrial Policy for the 1990s*, Report of the Industrial Policy Review Group, Dublin 1992, p.75–6.

[3] Michael Dargan, *Some issues facing the commercial state-sponsored bodies in Ireland, Administration 2*, 1987, p.123–4.

[4] *A Time for Change*, p.41.

9. The European Dimension

Brendan Halligan

IT WAS IN 1960 that I first heard Professor Patrick Lynch argue that there was no such thing as an Irish economy. As an economics student at the time, I was outraged at the proposition that what we assumed to be an independent economy was nothing more than a region of the British. However, outrage cannot outlast the facts, and his thesis was just too compelling when the realities were dispassionately analysed. So I quickly swallowed my nationalist pride and accepted an argument which has remained with me ever since as a luminous insight not only into the nature of the Irish economy, but into Irish society itself. That insight is the point of departure for this paper.

There is little need to rehearse the realities which underlay the Lynch thesis, save to measure the changes which have taken place in just one lifetime and then draw conclusions for the future. The strongest corroborative evidence was our dependence on Britain for international trade. Over 70 per cent of exports were to the adjoining island, confirming the point that this trade was inter-regional in character rather than international. Labour mobility was such that most Irish families had at least one member in Britain. We had no independent currency since the exchange rate was determined in London. Irish agriculture was a commodity supplier to the UK market with the inevitable corollary of low prices. Apart from a few commercial semi-state corporations and private companies sheltered from external competition, manufacturing in Ireland was mainly in the hands of British-owned subsidiaries. The long-term economic effect was that Irish growth rates were simply a function of the British, and since theirs weren't particularly buoyant throughout the century, neither were ours.

However, there were other significant consequences flowing from this essentially neocolonialist relationship. Ireland was still dominated by British, or more precisely English, values and attitudes, and we belonged to an Anglocentric world in which English language and culture predominated. Our contact with and knowledge of continental Europe was minimal. That would have been bad enough, given that British society had lost most of the inner dynamism which had made it the greatest power for much of the nineteenth century, but we suffered from a further colonial legacy which directly impeded the development of our economy. At the time Professor Lynch was shocking his naïve students into reality, we had no native entrepreneurial class worthy of the name. By entrepreneurship I mean more than the business pursuit of profit. I include the energy and determination to make things happen at any level in a sphere.

The most enduring legacy of colonialism is its impact on the spirit of enterprise, because the relationship between the conquerors and the conquered requires that initiative be comprehensively crushed, and remain so. While this can be beneficial to the imperial interests of the colonisers it is inimical to the national interests of the colonised. Passivity can degenerate into fatalism and the communal belief that things will never change, except for the worse, can thus become a self-fulfilling prophecy. Fatalism is the greatest enemy of progress and can bite so deeply that a society will come to resist change and resent success. Those who are old enough to remember the Ireland of the 1950s will, I am sure, recognise these characteristics as typical of the conservative society in which they then lived and from which, it was said, the young, energetic and ambitious fled at the first opportunity.

The Irish economy also suffered from another major

deficiency in that the stock of capital was woefully inadequate to fund infrastructure and industrial development. The rationale for colonialism is that the territories under imperial control should be bled of income, with retained earnings accumulated in the so-called mother country, and this had been applied with particular vigour to the Ireland of the nineteenth century. So, the colonial legacy was not just an impoverishment of the spirit, but of the material as well. Ireland embarked on its independence as a poor country with no industrial tradition and without the means to embark upon economic development.

Little wonder then that the Ireland of Patrick Lynch's insight was one of stagnation, with the major price in human terms being paid through a continuous haemorrhage of emigration which by the late 1950s had swollen to a flood tide. In terms of this series' title, the Irish economy always had a jobs crisis, and to react to the current one as if it were something unique is to deny the realities of our own historical formation and, worse still, to arrive at the wrong policy conclusions. There is nothing new in our failure to provide anything remotely approaching full employment, it was always so. Whether it will continue to be so is the question I have been asked to address in the context of the European dimension.

Why then have I taken so long to analyse what might be called 'The Jobs Crisis – the UK Dimension'? My response is that unless we understand where we have come from, we will never understand where we are now, and, more importantly, where we might be heading. The place from which we have come is that of a classic neocolonialist society as exemplified by the Ireland of 30 years ago. Where we are now is a society in transition which Professor Anthony Clare recently likened to that of adolescence, with all its attendant enthusiasms and immaturity. Where we might be heading is a matter for individual judgment, but my own belief is that we are evolving into a society typical of the small successful Northern European countries, although with an overlay of the Latin temperament. Substantial change has self-evidently taken place over the past three decades and, while the underlying factors are complex, our involvement in the European Community has been central to both its pace and direction. This point is crucial, as the following examples demonstrate.

Of the major changes which have taken place against the bench-mark of 1960, the most striking is the way we now view the world. The focus may still be Anglo-centric to some extent, for that is unavoidable in terms of language, geography and culture, but the geo-political centre of our immediate universe is switching from London to Brussels, and indeed to Paris and Bonn. This process has brought positive psychological benefits in its train which, in terms of their impact on economic development, arguably exceed in value the financial transfers we receive from the European Community. This had been foreseen by Euro-enthusiasts in the 1960s, when arguing in favour of Irish entry into the EEC.

On the level of the more tangible, the first consequence of note is the diversification of our trading relations so that our current pattern of international trade at last merits the use of the prefix, international. The second has been the ending of the feudal relationship of the Irish pound with sterling through our membership of the EMS, although the more cynical could counter that all we have done is swap the Bank of England for the Bundesbank. But even the most cynical could not deny that Irish agriculture has gained immeasurably from participation in the Common Agricultural Policy. Taken together, these three elements of change, trade, finance and agriculture, have combined to lessen substantially our economic dependence on Britain, while transforming our economic relations with the rest of the EC. The Irish economy may still be a regional one but it is evolving into a region of a different economic entity which is larger, more dynamic and conducive to our long-term interests.

The second major change is in the ethos of Irish society itself which is at present marked by an energy and self-reliance greater than at any time this century. The proof is all around us in many forms, in particular the local and voluntary organisations which so impressed President Robinson on her campaign trail. But from an economist's point of view the most significant has been the emergence of an entrepreneurial class in business. The evidence for that too exists, even if some of it is less than salutary.

For a people who are still subject to bouts of periodic mass depression, it is a necessary corrective to emphasise the business successes of the past 30 years and to use them as a pointer to the future. They include large companies with wide international connections, like Smurfit, CRH and Glen Dimplex, the five big co-ops which have transformed the dairy sector, the small- and medium-sized enterprises which compete in European and other markets, the intelligence-based services sector and, dare I say it, the various commercial semi-states which have successfully diversified their products, services and markets. The entrepreneur, as distinct from the manager, is no longer a *rara avis* but a flourishing species, if not yet sufficiently numerous.

The entrepreneur did not, of course, spontaneously appear on the scene, like a space traveller being beamed up onto the starship *Enterprise*. It was a slow cumulative process and the causal factors were many; generational change, citizenship of the global village, ease of mobility and the rise in the overall level of education. These influences still prevail and, if anything, are intensifying in their impact on the collective psyche of those who were once dismissed as the mere Irish. The overall effect of this multifaceted change is that the Lynch thesis no longer holds true. Something new has emerged. The era of stagnation is over and neocolonialism is ending. We are a society with a hybrid culture moving towards the heart of modern Europe, and the process is ongoing.

The interested observer will have realised that social change has mainly coincided with our membership of the EC. This year marks the twentieth anniversary of our accession to membership and is an appropriate point at which to reflect on how it has influenced individual behaviour and the management of our collective affairs. The economic benefits are clear enough, but the psychological advantages are a little more elusive although of greater importance in the long run. Continuous exposure to the politics and economics of other Europeans has had a beneficial effect not only on our self-image, but on our self-development. In terms of self-image we have come to realise that we can be as good as the best. Business people know this to be true of themselves and their products. Public officials and politicians recognise that they can play a role greater than our size would warrant in shaping and managing the EC. All this has had a purgative effect on the fatalism which had robbed us of initiative, energy and ambition. An enterprise culture has emerged and is growing in strength.

In terms of self-development, learning from other Europeans has been one of the more profound benefits from being involved in the Community. To me, the most influential has been the movement away from the British model of a conflictual society to a Continental one based on consensus. The Programme for Economic and Social Progress is expressly based on the social market as practised in most Community and EFTA countries, and would have been unattainable had we remained locked in the Anglophone world of Thatcherism and Reaganism instead of participating in the Community. Its implementation, and that of its precursor, the Programme for National Recovery, has done more to transform Irish politics, business, public finances, competitiveness, industrial relations and our institutional framework than any other innovation since the Second World War, and its origin lies in learning how societies and economies other than the British are organised and managed. The PESP now provides the institutional base on which a full-employment economy can be built. In summary, the European dimension of our collective experience these past 20 years has been a catalyst and agent for change, economically, socially and psychologically.

The key question is whether the Europeanisation of Irish society can be further accelerated, because if there is to be a solution to the jobs crisis, then it lies in Ireland becoming a fully paid-up member of the European economy. And that unavoidably brings us to the difficult part of the paper where one must hazard the dangers of policy prescription. I do so on the basis of the analysis I have just offered of Irish society, a society which I regard as *sui generis* in the development of modern Europe, and with the focus on the long term because the problems remain so great that they are not susceptible to a quick fix. The solution does not lie, for example, in tinkering with the tax system, but in a root and branch reform of Irish society which will take at least a generation to achieve. Any other approach is Utopian. As a people we have been poor at taking the long view and ensuring that national policies mutually reinforce each other in terms of objectives. What we need above all is what planners call policy efficiency, and the following proposals seek to present such a schema premised on the primary objectives of integrating as fast as possible into Europe and strengthening the spirit of enterprise and innovation.

The starting point for a national development strategy should be to see ourselves as much European as we are Irish. That vision is not yet as strongly articulated as it should be, and while a vision might seem to belong more to poetry than to economics, the lesson from best practice in the corporate world is that the planning process must begin by shaping a vision which is simple, intelligible and arresting. As an insight into the mechanics of inducing change it reminds us that any collectivity needs widely shared values and goals if it is to transform itself for the better. Change always involves pain and is invariably confronted by inertia. The energy and stamina necessary to endure the one and overcome the other are only generated when a leadership spells out the goals to be achieved and the benefits to be derived. Nothing could be more practical in terms of economic development than engaging in speculation by which we envision our common future as lying at the heart of Europe. National policy for ending the jobs crisis should be based on the over-riding principle that, from now on, the Irish economy is to be managed and structured as a region of an integrated European economy.

This would be consistent with the objectives of the Internal Market since membership implies that the various
national economies are destined to become regions of one
large single economy in which the laws of comparative advantage are to be given full effect. The logical consequence
of regarding ourselves as European would be to redefine our
home market as the EC, as well as EFTA. If we widen our
concept of the home market to encompass practically all of
the European mainland, then we must have the means of
participating within it so that our goods and services move
at the lowest cost and greatest speed. Demonstrably, that is
not yet the case.

Our internal communications are lamentable. For example, we have the smallest motorway network in the Community and our national rail system has fallen into decay.
Our external systems are not much better. Sea linkages with
the Continent are costly and inefficient, the ports are undeveloped, there is no national sea carrier and the penalties
of peripherality have largely remained unaddressed. This is
all the more disturbing in circumstances where just-in-time
delivery systems are becoming the industrial norm and
where the retail trade demands rapid and reliable service to
reduce the costs of holding stocks.

What we need with great urgency is to implement an integrated transport strategy which minimises the disadvant-
ages of distance from the core of our new home market. We
need a fully developed road and rail system by the end of
the century which feeds into our ports. We need to designate
those ports which are to be the main points of access to the
market, equip them with the most modern handling facilities and service them with efficient shipping schedules. We
need, too, an air bridge to the heart of our new home market.

There is a disjunction between the various assertions of
the importance of the Internal Market and the policy response in removing the external diseconomies imposed
upon Irish business by the exigencies of geography. If we do

not establish efficient lines of communications by air and sea
with the rest of our continent, then Irish business will lose
out on its opportunities and the jobs crisis will continue. It
follows that the first operational priority of mentally reposi-
tioning ourselves at the heart of Europe is to equip Irish
business with the means of physically doing likewise. For an
economy which exports some 80 per cent of its output, this
is hardly an extravagant demand.

If we psychologically reposition ourselves at Europe's
heart's core, then we must confront another challenge, for
we are not only separated from it by water, but by language.
It has been said that to have a second language is to have a
second mind, a profound insight which reminds us that language is an integral part of culture. It is also said that in
business you buy in your own language but sell in the customer's, an interesting piece of sales psychology. Taken together, these two sayings provide the second agenda item
for national action, that of equipping ourselves with a range
of linguistic skills comparable to the Dutch or Scandina-
vians. These small countries prove that a native tongue
which no one else understands need not constitute a barrier
to trade; on the contrary, their experience suggests that linguistic isolation can act as a powerful stimulus to master the
languages of one's markets.

To some extent, this is what we did in the nineteenth
century by learning English. We will have to repeat that
Darwinian adaptation of the species if we are to survive
amongst the fittest in the new environment of a single European economy, and be capable of moving with the same ease
and fluency in Berlin, Paris, Rome or Madrid as we currently
do in London. The goal will have to be achieved in one generation, and it will have to be done clinically with an eye on
where our main markets are likely to be.

The portfolio of languages taught in schools should
mirror the markets in which we sell or intend to sell, much
as a good corporate treasurer will cover the currencies in
which a business trades. Furthermore, the teaching of modern European languages should begin in primary school in

accordance with best pedagogic practice. If every student emerging from second level had reasonable command over two other languages, then the communications barrier between us and the Internal Market would be removed with increasing economic benefits. However, from what I said earlier about the need to create an enterprise culture, you can understand that I regard the psychological benefits to be gained from language learning as being of even greater importance in integrating ourselves into Europe.

What then can we sell into our new home market on the basis of efficient physical communications and expert language skills? I believe that the answer lies within the general logic upon which the Treaty of Rome is based and which the Single European Act expands; that free competition between the economies of Europe will force each to specialise in those goods and services in which it enjoys the greatest comparative advantage. The truth of the proposition is as incontestable as it is unavoidable, and it should encourage us to examine again what we believe ours to be. For my part, I would like to posit a modern version of the Land League's demands, popularly known as the 'three Fs'. In this case, the 'three Fs' are Food, Fisheries and Forestry, and Europe can play a central role in simultaneously developing all three.

With respect to food, virtually everything has been said, but too little accomplished. Suffice it to say that our perennial weaknesses are in marketing, distribution and product development, a point made by the Telesis Report a decade ago. A country with our natural advantages of soil and climate should have four or five major players in the world food market, but we do not, for the reasons I outlined at the beginning. The medium-term requirement is to develop a number of internationally recognisable brands to act as umbrellas under which our food producers could sell. Creating those brands, as Kerrygold proves, can bring handsome rewards, but is enormously expensive and beyond the capacity of most existing companies. It would make more sense in terms of value added (and, therefore, jobs) if state support for industry concentrated less on physical assets and more on brand and market development, a point particularly pertinent to the meat sector which is so heavily dependent on intervention buying and the generosity, as well as the patience, of the German taxpayer.

At least it can be said of the dairy sector that a start has been well made, but we are only at the beginning of a fishing industry appropriate to an island with 17 per cent of the Community's fishing waters, and we have hardly begun in forestry, where we languish at the bottom of the Community's league table for the percentage of land under forest. To gauge the potential of either, one need only look at Norway and Finland. Employment comes not just from primary production, but from creating value added products which spin off service industries, which in turn can spawn standalone industries, such as engineering. Due to the absence of an enterprise culture we have lost out on that sort of development, but the scale of the structural funds over the next seven years is such that both industries could be developed to the point of self-sustaining growth. As with food, the market opportunities are there but the realisation of their potential depends on putting the proper strategies in place and then, of course, implementing them. Irish entrepreneurship should be let loose on the 'three Fs' with the assistance of the structural funds. Should that be done, then I have little doubt that 30 years from now a jobs crisis in Ireland will be the subject of historical research rather than a subject for contemporary political action.

I would like to advance two support strategies, but only briefly because the arguments by now are so familiar. 'Educate that you may be free,' advised Thomas Davis, to which we might add, 'that you may prosper'. It is significant, surely, that Germany, Austria and Switzerland have all invested heavily in technical education for generations. These successful examples of investing in people, the other great natural resource, have caught the imagination of the Irish Congress of Trade Unions and a recommendation to introduce the German system here by the end of the decade figured amongst their top priorities for the use of the next *tranche* of the structural funds. Were that to be done, then it would provide us with the skills on which a natural-resource-based economy could develop over a generation. We would have a total education system equal to the best. No further elaboration is necessary, just action.

The other issue is that of research and development. Persuasive evidence exists regarding the correlation between the level of expenditure on research and development and economic growth. Our own expenditure is amongst the lowest in the EC and we do not yet have a science and technology strategy which would foster innovation. We are still light years away from making this country a centre of excellence in both basic and applied research and, more particularly, in product development. This is especially true of indigenous industry and we need to emulate best European practice with urgency. The structural funds should be consciously employed to raise the level of expenditure to the EC norm by the end of the decade, with particular focus on developing value added products derived from our natural resources. Were this to be done systematically, it would provide us with the critical mass upon which an efficient industrial sector could be based, and so ensure a high employment regional economy.

The final strategy proposal relates to finance, the life-blood of the economy. Here again, the European dimension is of benefit because the financial system on the Continent is generally different from the British model which we still operate here. The distinguishing characteristic of most European systems is that banks often take an equity stake in companies rather than concentrating exclusively on the provision of debt. This enables them, or causes them, to adopt a long view of corporate performance rather than the frantic short-term approach so typical of the City of London. From the viewpoint of this analysis the importance of a long-term relationship is that it reinforces the role of the entrepreneur by providing equity instead of debt, and judges performance over years rather than quarters.

The final building block in the construction of a European regional economy should be a reformed financial sector, particularly banking. I am aware that in the USA some economists are questioning the role of their financial institutions in promoting growth and that the same questions are being raised here, but to a much more limited extent. This should be encouraged because without this essential reform the entrepreneurial energy and managerial skills which now abound in Ireland will never realise their full potential, and the jobs crisis will continue.

One last reform is essential if we are to complete the Europeanisation of Ireland. That is the adoption of administrative structures which give real power to local communities and regions. Recent research has confirmed that there is a direct correlation between economic growth and the empowerment of local authorities. After 70 years of independence we still insist on using a highly centralised system more suitable to a colonial power than a free people. The consequent loss of communal and regional enterprise is no accident but a direct consequence of this choice. If we are intent on ending the jobs crisis, then a fundamental reform of local government, such as that undertaken in Denmark, must be effected in conjunction with the measures just outlined.

In summary, I have proposed that over a generation we consciously engineer a dynamic regional economy based on natural resources which is totally integrated into Europe, serviced by efficient communications, language proficiency, a skilled labour force, high investment in research and development and a reformed banking sector which supports indigenous entrepreneurs. I have argued that the institutional framework for long-term development based on social consensus is already in place. But to end the jobs crisis we also require a long-range strategy. We need a coherent policy framework formulated by Government, for economic growth does not happen by chance. It results from choices made at many levels, individual and corporate, regional and national. This last element has been notable mainly by its absence since independence.

The Telesis Report a decade ago commented that it was astounding that the Government was not involved directly in formulating and assessing development strategy. That remains the position. Perhaps the new Department of Enterprise and Employment marks a welcome departure by linking the two. Should this be the case, then, for the first time, there is a real cause for hope that Ireland will overcome the bitter legacy of history and enjoy a future long dreamed of but so far unattained.

10. The Keynesian Legacy

Brendan Walsh

INTELLECTUAL FASHION IN regard to the problem of unemployment changes. During the 1980s the dominance of Reaganite and Thatcherite ideas led some to believe that all that was needed to re-invigorate the economy was for the state to distance itself from the marketplace. The popular version of this doctrine went: 'Deregulate, denationalise, reduce public spending and taxes, make the social welfare system harsher, and the economy will grow faster and those who really want to work will be able to find jobs'. However, with the onset of recession in 1990 and unemployment increasing from a level that was already very high by historical standards, faith has declined in the ability of the economies of Europe to restore anything approaching 'full employment' unless an active role is played by government. Following the retirement of Mrs Thatcher as Prime Minister in Britain, the inauguration of President Clinton in the United States and the formation of a new Government with Labour Party participation in this country, the mood has changed. While there has been no return to the uncritical interventionism of earlier years, a form of Keynesianism is enjoying a comeback.

To gain a perspective on the problem of unemployment, and the conflicting views that exist as to how it should be dealt with, it is helpful to review the changes that have taken place in the way economists have analysed it over the years.

Until the second quarter of the twentieth century economists had surprisingly little to say about unemployment. It was recognised that some workers – dockers or casual

labourers, for example – were prone to periodic unemployment, while others, such as bank clerks and university pro-
fessors, were not. Economists believed that unemployment
rose as boom gave way to slump, but quickly fell during the
recovery. They wrote about *Lapses from Full Employment.*[1]
Contrary to what Marx had predicted, the evidence did not
suggest that unregulated market economies tended to generate worsening crises with persistent and widespread unemployment.

Changing realities changed the way economists looked
at the problem. After the First World War, in Britain hundreds of thousands of workers were demobilised. At first the
economy coped well with the task of re-absorbing them into
civilian employment. Output and employment boomed until
1920, but the boom was followed by the most severe recession that Britain had experienced in a century. When stability returned in 1923 it was on the basis of a 10 per cent rate
of unemployment. The economy limped along for the rest of
the 1920s as the traditional industries – coal mining, ship-
building, steel-making and textiles – tried to cope with the
problems of excess capacity, fragmentation, union–management conflicts, and, above all, unemployment.

The emergence of persistent, large-scale unemployment
in the 1920s forced economists to confront the problem and
to ask why so many people were condemned to remain
more or less permanently without work and in poverty, despite the glaring unmet needs that were evident on all sides.
In the ensuing debate themes emerged that have remained
at the forefront of discussions on unemployment ever since.

Orthodox opinion in the 1920s laid much of the blame
for unemployment at the door of wage rates that were too
high in relation to what employers could afford to pay. This
diagnosis led straightforwardly to the conclusion that workers should accept wage cuts until the labour market cleared.
However, John Maynard Keynes argued that while a depression could force firms to cut prices as they competed for con-
sumer spending, the day was gone when unemployed workers would respond to rising unemployment by accepting

lower wages. The power of trades unions and universal suf-
frage prevented a return to this nineteenth-century sort of
adjustment. Interestingly, Keynes also laid some of the
blame on the dole, which placed a floor under the wages
that workers would accept. In a radio talk in 1930 he said:

> The existence of the dole undoubtedly diminishes the pressure
> on the individual man to accept a rate of wages or a kind of
> employment which is not just what he wants or what he is
> used to.[2]

British industry and its failure to adjust to the post-war realities also received some of the blame for unemployment in
the 1920s. While Keynes, like many academics, took a dim
view of business as a career and money-making as a motive,
he believed that the amateurishness of British businessmen
was part of the reason why British industry was doing so
badly. He thought that the British coal industry was 'deca-
dent' and its owners 'halfwitted', while the owners of the
Lancashire textile mills were 'old and obstinate' and their
behaviour 'suicidal'. But he acknowledged the problems
created by cheap imports from Japan, which threatened the
British textile industry with extinction, and the difficulties
caused by the traditional attitudes of British workers, which
made them prefer to remain unemployed in their local communities rather than to move to the south of England where
new industries were creating jobs. He drafted a report in
1927 which urged the Government to assist industry in an
age of transition with subsidies to training, labour mobility
and what we would now call research and development. He
urged the Liberal Party, in which he was active, to experiment with 'all kinds of new partnerships between the state
and private enterprise'.[3] He was in favour of more spending
on public works, citing the expansion of the telephone network as an example of a worthwhile project.

On a note that will be familiar to an Irish audience,
Keynes included population growth among the factors con-
tributing to the high rate of unemployment. Like his pre-
decessor at Cambridge, Robert Malthus, he believed in his

early days that 'the problem of unemployment is ... in part a problem of population'.[4] He pointed out that the British employable population was growing by between 100,000 and 200,000 a year and he believed that 'we shall not be able to employ the whole employable population except at the very top of periodic booms'. The solution lay in a great improvement in industrial competitiveness and, in the longer run, the practice of birth control.

Finally, in 1925 Keynes ridiculed the Bank of England and the Treasury for restoring the pound to the gold standard at its 1918 parity. He believed that the deflation required as the economy tried to adjust to an overvalued exchange rate contributed to the persistence of high unemployment. When sterling was taken off gold in 1931 Keynes rejoiced that Britain had broken her 'gold fetters' and was free to pursue a more sensible policy.

Thus, many of the explanations for high unemployment that are still invoked to this day – excessive wage levels, over-generous unemployment benefits, poor management, the rapid growth of the labour force and an overvalued exchange rate – can be found in Keynes' writing during the 1920s. And many of the remedies he advocated – public works, training programmes, aids to industry, slower population growth and maintaining a competitive exchange rate – are still relevant today.

These are *not*, however, the ideas that we think of as characteristically Keynesian. The Great Depression profoundly affected his thinking about the problem of unemployment and led him to formulate a wholly different view of it. The financial and economic collapse in America at the end of the 1920s shattered his belief that the problem could be cured by minor adjustments in economic policy. As the American economy plunged into depression, he came to believe that what was happening reflected deep-seated flaws in the capitalist system. His desire to correct these flaws and prevent capitalism from being replaced by a totalitarianism of the right or of the left led him to undertake a fundamental critique of traditional economics. He concluded that unemployment should no longer be viewed primarily as a reflection of workers pricing themselves out of jobs or the rigidities of declining industries; instead the fundamental problem was the inadequacy of effective demand – too much savings and too little spending. A wage cut would not price workers back into non-existent jobs, in fact it could make matters worse by reducing the amount of money in circulation. The villains of the piece were prudent savers who discouraged investment by not spending their income and businessmen who were too pessimistic about the future to launch bold new projects.

This type of reasoning was an attack on core Victorian values. It rejected the traditional view of savings as a mainspring of economic progress and glorified the spendthrift as fulfilling a useful social role. A puritanical lifestyle kept money out of circulation, whilst luxurious living gave employment. Keynes went so far as to state in a radio broadcast in 1931: 'Whenever you save five shillings, you put a man out of work'. He regretted that the Victorian entrepreneurs, whose sheer animal spirits had covered the country with railways and factories, had been succeeded by a cautious generation that preferred putting money on deposit at compound interest to genuine risk-taking.

Keynes concluded that because households saved too much and businessmen were reluctant to invest, the state should accept direct responsibility for organising some investment. Of course, the civil servants in the Treasury objected that this would discourage private enterprise. To counter this objection Keynes, in a famous passage, proposed that the Treasury 'fill old bottles with bank notes, bury them at suitable depths in disused coal-mines and leave it to private enterprise on the well-tried principles of laissez faire to dig the notes up again'. At least such a public-works programme could not be accused of competing with the private sector!

The key propositions that have come to be known as Keynesian are, then, a view of savings as a vice rather than a virtue, a belief that the public sector should undertake capital projects that would not be profitable according to the criteria of private sector investment appraisal, and advocacy of spending for the sake of recirculating income and putting the unemployed back to work.

Keynes was struck by the idea that an initial outlay of public money would pass from hand to hand 'perhaps 20 times in the course of a year', each time generating additional spending and employment. The final effect on incomes would be some multiple of the initial injection of purchasing power. This was the origin of the concept of the multiplier, which became a standard tool in the kit of economists and is still widely invoked to justify new proposals for spending public money. Keynes himself settled for a multiplier of about 2 under British conditions, somewhat higher in America, rather than the much higher figures that were to be used in popularised versions of his theory. None the less, there seemed to be here the promise of 'something for nothing', a lunch which, if not exactly free, was half-price!

However, Keynes was not a Keynesian in the crude sense in which this term came to be used in later years. He always recognised the importance of private-sector investment and accepted that persistent budget deficits and over-ambitious schemes of public works could undermine investors' confidence. His agenda did not include thorough-going state control of the economy or the centralisation of investment. He was more conscious than many who invoked his ideas in later years of the need to preserve efficiency and freedom whilst tackling the problem of unemployment.

The 'Keynesian revolution' occurred on two levels. First, there was the intellectual challenge to mainstream economic thinking. Second, there was the justification of a more active role for the state as a regulator of aggregate spending.

On the first level, Keynes revolutionised the way economists looked at the problem of unemployment. After the appearance of *The General Theory*[5] in 1936, it was no longer possible to relegate unemployment to a minor topic in the study of economics. Keynes' ideas were quickly systematised and became familiar to an ever-growing population of students of economics. However, in the 1960s an intellectual counter-revolution gathered momentum, led by economists in the Austrian and Chicago tradition, among whom Milton Friedman is the most famous. Macro-economics as taught today is a synthesis of these different views of how the economy works.

Keynesian impact on economic policy is more difficult to assess. In 1937 Neville Chamberlain's Government drafted plans to borrow on a modest scale for rearmament. Keynes gave a cautious welcome to this change of policy on the part of the Conservatives. Within two years the problem of wartime finance had displaced from centre stage that of unemployment. As the war drew to a close, he devoted the last years of his life to working on the establishment of the International Monetary Fund and the Bretton Woods system of fixed exchange rates. The problem of unemployment, so dominant in the 1920s and 1930s, faded into the background.

It was war-time spending and post-war reconstruction, rather than Keynesian economics, that led to the massive expansion of the role of the state in the economy throughout the western world during and after the Second World War. In Ireland, the development of a Public Capital Programme during the late 1940s was not an exercise in Keynesian economics, but an attempt to convince American lenders that we would make good use of the loans offered under the Marshall Plan. Nor did the famous *Programme for Economic Expansion* in 1958 endorse a Keynesian agenda. The idea that a current budget deficit should be incurred in order to stimulate the economy was not entertained until the 1970s, when politicians became convinced that the correct way to tackle the problem of unemployment was through tax cuts and increased public spending. It is strange that the conversion to Keynesianism came at a time when real wages were rising rapidly and for the first time in our history large numbers of people were returning to the country to fill the available employment opportunities. The 1978 budget – the most expansionary in the history of the state – was justified by the Keynesian argument that increased government spending would be the first stage of a process, the later stages of which would consist of the increased private-sector spending stimulated by the initial expansion. It is ironic that Keynes should have warned, in an oft-quoted passage, that 'practical men, who believe themselves exempt from any intellectual influences, are usually the slaves of some defunct economist'. Keynes himself was the defunct economist who enslaved our policy makers in the 1970s.

The results of this experiment in crude Keynesianism were disappointing. We enjoyed a spurt of exceptionally rapid economic growth in 1978 and 1979, but this was followed by no fewer than eight consecutive years of below average growth. The rate of unemployment fell to just over 7 per cent in 1979, but it increased steadily over the next eight years, reaching 17.5 per cent in 1987 and falling only to 13.5 per cent in 1990 after three years of rapid growth, before beginning to rise again with the onset of the current recession. The overhang of debt and interest payments from the fiscal expansion of the 1970s still looms large in the budgetary arithmetic facing the Government in 1993.

The failure of the expansionary fiscal policies implemented in the late 1970s permanently to lower the rate of unemployment led to the emergence of a new view, or more accurately a return to the older view, of the unemployment problem. It came to be widely accepted by economists that while the level of aggregate demand affects the rate of unemployment in the short run, it does not explain, for example, why the average rate of unemployment is more than twice as high in Ireland as in the United States or why so many of our unemployed have been out of work for months or even years, whereas unemployment in America is predominantly of short duration.

To understand these aspects of the unemployment problem we have to analyse how labour markets work and why they often don't work. The analytical tools that were used in the 1920s, rather than those fashioned by Keynes in the 1930s, are the ones relevant to this task. To appreciate how far the economics profession has moved from the Keynesian emphasis on a deficiency of aggregate demand as an explanation for unemployment, it is instructive to examine a book published in 1991 by three prominent British economists.[6] The book is dedicated to 'the millions who suffer through want of work'. In contrast to Keynes' *General Theory*, which contains only one diagram, a few equations and even fewer statistics, this book runs to over 600 pages and is studded with diagrams, equations and tables of data. It is an encyclopaedia of modern research into the problem of unemployment. It concludes with a chapter devoted to 'Policies to Cut Unemployment'. While the authors accept that a fall in the level of demand is the usual cause of a rise in unemployment, they emphasise that the way the labour market works determines how much unemployment rises and how long it stays high. A general expansion of aggregate demand is not seen as a realistic way out of a recession. Moreover, policies such as a general increase in public-sector employment, early retirement and work sharing are believed more likely to impoverish a country than to reduce unemployment.

Most of the policies the authors advocate relate to changes in the unemployment benefit system or in the way unions and employers bargain about wages. Their first conclusion, based on detailed research into the behaviour of unemployment in 19 OECD countries, is that 'unemployment will fall if unemployment benefits are of limited duration and subject to stronger job-search tests'.[7] They link this recommendation to a proposal to spend more on training and placement, and even guaranteed public-sector employment for the long-term unemployed, in order to avoid the hardship that would be caused if benefits were curtailed without compensating policies. They also favour subsidising the employment of hard-to-employ groups and centralised wage bargaining between unions and employers, with tax cuts as rewards for pay moderation.

Reading these recommendations, we are returned to a pre-Keynesian world, 55 years after the publication of *The General Theory*. We see that after a fairly brief flirtation with the idea that governments could cure unemployment by spending their way out of stagnation, orthodox economic opinion has swung back to the views that were fashionable in the 1920s.

This is also evident from the fact that, even though we face a sharply deteriorating economic situation in Europe today, few economists would endorse a large-scale fiscal stimulus as a way of preventing further increases in the unemployment rate. No Irish economist has urged the new Government, which has given the problem of unemployment a high priority in its *Programme for Government*, to embark on tax cuts and increased spending in order to bring the rate of unemployment down. The failed experiment of the 1970s has made us profoundly sceptical of this approach. Keynesianism, to the extent that it is enjoying a comeback, is limited to advocating that high levels of government spending and taxation are almost inevitable and may even help promote economic growth.

None the less, many commentators continue to claim that active policies have not been pursued with sufficient vigour to alleviate unemployment in Ireland. Indeed it is common to denounce successive Governments for failing to take the problem seriously. But the reality is that most options have been tried and found wanting under Irish conditions. In fact, it is difficult to identify any approach to the problem of unemployment within the power of the state that has not been tried, and pushed to its limits, in Ireland. In addition to the active fiscal policy that was pursued in the 1970s, numerous measures have been undertaken to promote economic development and employment. The private sector was rigorously protected from foreign competition for over 30 years, from the 1930s to the 1960s; the long list of state-owned companies established since Independence remains largely in place, despite the tide of privatisation that swept over the western world in the 1980s; as protectionism was dismantled, a vast amount of taxpayers' money was spent on grants and other aids to encourage foreign and indigenous investment in industry; spending on a variety of other schemes to create employment and reduce unemployment has grown steadily and in recent years Governments have entered into a series of pacts with unions and employers with the intent of fostering employment and lowering unemployment. In fact, I am tempted to remark that the only policy untried in Ireland is that of withdrawing from the economy and letting businesses and households get on with the job of creating employment.

There is, however, one Keynesian prescription that received too little attention in recent Irish policy making. This is his emphasis on maintaining a competitive exchange rate in order to alleviate unemployment. Until 1979 this was not really an issue in Ireland; the sterling link removed the exchange rate from the list of available policy instruments. However, the Irish authorities' decision to join the European Monetary System in 1979 led almost immediately to the breaking of the sterling link. Since then we have been grappling with the implications of trying to remain in the exchange rate mechanism of the EMS, while at the same time maintaining a competitive exchange rate relative to sterling. The sharp depreciation of sterling in September 1992 posed this dilemma in an extreme manner. It was decided to hold the value of the Irish pound in terms of the German mark, even though this involved a sudden loss of competitiveness in our main export markets and extraordinarily high interest rates. This policy undoubtedly cost jobs and raised unemployment, but it was rationalised on the grounds that in the longer run it would lead to financial stability and faster growth in employment. In the transition period the whole economy would have to adjust to a strong currency – a slow and painful process, involving higher unemployment – similar to the one Keynes described after Britain went back on the gold standard in 1925.

In the debate on Irish exchange-rate policy, there were frequent references to the 'economic fundamentals'. We were assured that they were sound in Ireland and gave no grounds for lowering the value of the currency. Usually included in the list of fundamentals were the rate of inflation, the Government's budget deficit and the balance of payments surplus. Omitted from the list were the level of interest rates, which rose to record levels during the currency crisis, the rate of economic growth, which fell sharply, the level of employment, which has shown no net increase over the last 15 years, and the unprecedented rate of unemployment.

It is curious that trade unionists and others who would regard themselves as Keynesians lined up behind a strong exchange-rate policy of the type that was ridiculed by Keynes in the 1920s. Many factors – mistakes of economic analysis, national pride, an irrational attachment to a particular exchange rate – accounted for this. As a result, financial fundamentals became a fetish and employment creation was displaced from the priority among the goals of economic policy that it should always have under Irish conditions.

Footnotes

[1] This is the title given to a book by Keynes' colleague, Arthur Pigou.

[2] Cited in Robert Skidelsky, *John Maynard Keynes: The Economist as Saviour 1920–1937*, Macmillan, London, 1992, p.347.

[3] *Loc. cit.*, p.264.

[4] *Loc. cit.*, p.149.

[5] J.M. Keynes, *The General Theory of Employment, Interest and Money*, Macmillan, London, 1936.

[6] Richard Layard, Stephen Nickell and Richard Jackman, *Unemployment: Macroeconomic Performance and the Labour Market*, Oxford University Press, 1991.

[7] *Loc. cit.*, p.508.

11. A Business Response

Professor David Kennedy

THE GRAVITY OF our unemployment crisis can be illustrated in a number of different ways. 20 per cent of our potential workforce is unemployed. Over 100,000 of our people have been on the Live Register for longer than one year. Over 50,000 have been continuously unemployed for more than three years.

I recently read a report which brought home to me the underlying reality of this problem far more effectively than the bare statistics. It was a research project on the wide range of social problems encountered by adolescents in Dublin today and covered such depressing areas as family breakdown, illicit drug and alcohol abuse, sexual problems and high crime rates. The single largest cause of these problems was identified as unemployment, not surprisingly when one considers that unemployment rates of between 60 per cent and 80 per cent are prevalent in many parts of our towns and cities. The marginalisation of so many communities raises important moral issues of social justice as well as the more obvious social and economic problems, not to mention the underlying threat to the future stability of society.

If one believes, as I do, that it is business and not Government that creates jobs, what changes in the present approach and policies should be considered? What is the business response to this challenge or indeed should there be a specific business response? In this lecture I will argue that business has a responsibility to generate national wealth and that it has obligations to the society in which it operates, as well as rights. I will also argue that if companies are to survive in the longer term, their first priority must be to be highly competitive and efficient by the demanding standards of today's international markets. I will also suggest that more than this is needed. Business operates in a national framework where industrial, social, economic, educational, and taxation policies influence its ability to create employment. Accordingly, a long-term integrated strategy is needed to bring these separate strands together to address the problem effectively.

PART OF the difficulty we are facing is that, in today's world, high rates of economic growth do not necessarily lead to a corresponding increase in employment. This problem is likely to become even more pronounced in the future, especially in manufacturing industry. A prominent European industrialist recently estimated that the proportion of Europe's labour force employed in manufacturing industries will fall from about 35 per cent today to 25 per cent in ten years time, and to 15 per cent a decade later. Over the next decade we may well see in manufacturing industry a replay of what has happened in agriculture since the Second World War, where improved methods of productivity have led to heavy job losses in rural communities.

It is easy to become even more apocalyptic about the future, when one considers other developments on the international scene. The breaking down of national barriers and increasing globalisation of industries mean that international firms will find it easy to locate their manufacturing activities in the areas of lowest cost, whether these be in South-East Asia, in Eastern Europe or elsewhere.

There are many ways in which Irish society can be improved, and the recently published Programme for Government contains a number of excellent aspirations. However, the problem about having a lot of priorities is that they inevitably dilute one another. If we really believed as a community that unemployment was the overriding national priority, virtually all other objectives, however desirable, would be subordinated to that. A country in a national emergency, such as a war, marshals all of its national resources in order to survive and my first suggestion is that such a single-minded focus is needed today.

MOVING ON from the general to the particular, I would now like to consider the role of Irish business in job creation. Some ideologists would argue that the only responsibility of business is to safeguard the interests of shareholders and maximise their return on investment. This could imply that business has no responsibility for generating economic growth or for providing jobs within the community, other than as an indirect consequence of earning profits. Personally, I find such a concept unattractive. In society today, business is given legitimacy based on its ability to generate growth in the overall standard of living, by efficiently harnessing human, natural and financial resources. It does this by providing more and better goods and services at lower real prices, by employing more people in production at increasing real wages and by providing satisfactory returns to those who have entrusted their personal resources in the future prosperity of the business. In other words, business is an agent of society and has obligations and responsibilities as well as rights.

In their recent booklet on this subject, the Irish Catholic bishops focused on the balance that has to be struck between respect for the economic initiative of the individual and the right to work of everyone. They referred to a clear conviction that ownership of property carries a social mortgage 'in order that goods may serve the general purpose that God gave them'.[1]

However, it is dangerously easy to go from this point to arguing that the main function of business is to create jobs. In the first place, this ignores the fundamental responsibility of companies to safeguard and provide a return on the investments which have been entrusted to them. For the most part, today in Ireland, their shareholders are not wealthy individuals but rather insurance companies and pension funds who look after the long-term interests of all of us. Job creation that does not add to productive national wealth merely redistributes existing wealth.

Furthermore, business has an overriding obligation to be highly efficient in its use of resources and that includes human resources. To put it in simple terms, in today's global economy, companies which are not efficient will not survive. Many companies in Ireland have had to face up to the unpleasant task of reducing the size of their workforce in order to be able to continue to compete in demanding international markets. A number of companies which have failed to do so have gone out of business. The first obligation of any business to its stake-holders, whether owners or employees, is survival.

Waterford Glass has been in the headlines recently. All reasonable people will regret the substantial job losses which have occurred. Equally, however, it is perfectly clear that without these job losses the cost of their products would simply have remained uncompetitive. Production would either have had to cease totally or else be transferred outside Ireland to a cost environment in which it would be competitive. In either case, the core jobs which the business can support would also have been lost.

The task for Irish businesses today, particularly those operating in the exposed internationally-traded markets, is simple to describe but very demanding to achieve. *They have to operate at the highest international standards of efficiency in order to be able to compete effectively.* That is the only way in which they can earn sustainable profits and by which long-term job stability can be provided. I have no doubt that management in Waterford Glass and in many other Irish companies, have acted in the long-term interests, not only of their companies, but also of the community as a whole, by implementing difficult and painful redundancy programmes to ensure that they remained competitive.

There are some who would argue that our unemployment crisis can be blamed on failures of Irish business, but the facts do not support such a conclusion. Since 1986, there has actually been a small but steady growth in employment in Irish industry averaging some 1 per cent per annum. Industrial output has grown over the same period by an average of 8 per cent per annum. The fact that such a high growth of industrial output gives such a modest growth in jobs serves to underline the earlier point, that in today's industrial world, one needs to be able to run very fast in increasing output even to sustain existing job levels.

Irish industry has not only been increasing its output, but it has also become increasingly competitive internationally. In 1980, approximately half of our industrial output was sold within Ireland (including North and South) and 20 per cent went to mainland Europe. By 1990 the figure for domestic sales had gone down to 25 per cent, and the proportion exported to mainland Europe had doubled to 40 per cent. In other words, much of the recent growth has been in internationally-traded goods and services. In addition, it has largely come from established companies rather than from fresh IDA-supported foreign investment.

The reality is that there are many recent success stories from Irish companies. The challenge is to build on these success stories, to encourage Irish entrepreneurs to expand even further in the years ahead and for all of us to create a climate in which other investors and entrepreneurs will be encouraged to seek further opportunities. The pity is that in earlier decades we failed to create a broad indigenous industrial base to supplement our success in attracting efficient foreign investment.

Innovation and entrepreneurship are by no means confined to private industry. State-owned commercial enterprises have a proud record of generating ideas and actions for economic growth. Companies such as Aer Lingus, Bord na Móna and ESB have pioneered many successful innovations and should be encouraged to continue doing so. The orientation must, of course, be to operate as businesses, taking commercial decisions, and not as agents of government, creating artificial jobs.

THERE IS a limit to what business can do on its own to generate economic activity. As I have said, business operates within a framework where a range of industrial, economic and social policies all influence its ability to be successful. At the general level of national industrial policy, the commitment in the new Government Programme to implement the recommendations of the Culliton Report is welcome. This report has been positively received and its implementation should be a high priority. It focuses on the development of policies which will enable the creation of long-term viable employment by improving the competitiveness of Irish industry.

I would like to comment on some of the detailed areas of industrial policy covered in this report, but before doing so I would like to address the question as to how far national policy should go in direct intervention in industry. Should we consider not only implementing Culliton but even going somewhat further?

There is general agreement that Government can help business to generate economic activity by such policies as low public borrowing, low interest rates, favourable tax régimes, investment in education, in infrastructure and in certain sorts of research and development. The more controversial question is whether policies that seek to pick and protect winners should also be pursued. The Culliton Report does support the encouragement by Government of clusters of related industries and highlights, in particular, the potential of the food industry in Ireland.

However, a number of countries with successful industrial economies including Japan, France and Germany have had policies which appear to go much further. Specifically, in their own different ways, each of these countries has developed mechanisms to provide early warnings of industry decline and adopted active labour and regional policies to ease transitions from uncompetitive industries. Equally, they have been proactive in helping to restructure industry to take better advantage of growth opportunities. The new United States Administration is strongly committed to moving in this direction and the newly-appointed Chairman of the President's Council of Economic Advisors, Laura Tyson, is one of the country's leading advocates of active trade and industrial policies.

Opponents of such an approach can point with some justification to a number of spectacular failures where large sums of money were wasted. The development of the Concorde aircraft by the French and British Governments was a particular case in point. Equally, however, in a number of cases Government intervention has been crucial in enabling restructuring to occur. The Shannon hydroelectric scheme transformed our economy in the early decades of the state. The lesson would appear to be that the ability of Governments to pick winners is limited, but that Government can play a strong and constructive role in working with and through businesses to support long-term strategic developments. Interventionist policies by Government should not be condemned universally.

As a particular example, I believe that our Government should give a high priority to the development of Irish tourism, where there is significant potential for job creation. In the past a lot of lip service has been given to tourism while reducing the resources allocated to the industry for development. This is hardly consistent with proclaimed policies of supporting strategically important industries. The Government Programme does promise to implement the main recommendations of the recently published Report of the Tourism Task Force although regrettably remaining silent on one of its key recommendations, namely to change the current Shannon stopover policy.

NATIONAL EDUCATION and training policies are crucial to the success of industry and thus vital for the long-term success of job-creation policies. Skills and knowledge do constitute one of the few areas where an economy can command a differential competitive advantage. To a large extent competition in global markets today has become a competition between different educational systems.

In a number of respects our education and training system is meeting that challenge but it does have a number of defects. In particular, many of those who leave full-time education at the 16- to 18-year-old level do so without having acquired the skills necessary for productive employment. By and large, the present system caters very well for the top 30 per cent of academic performers, namely those who can expect to graduate well from a three- or four-year college degree programme. However, economic competitiveness for a country is at least as likely to be determined by the skill level of the workforce as a whole rather than by the academic achievements of the élite, and this is where we do have a particular problem.

The development of the vocational education system and regional technical colleges in Ireland in the late 1960s was intended to cater for students who do not respond well to abstract blackboard-and-chalk teaching and give them the skills for productive employment. However, today the majority of the students enrolled in comprehensive and community or vocational schools are pursuing academic-type subjects leading to the Leaving Certificate examination.

What has happened is a continuing drift away from vocational-type education to academic education: the exact reverse of what many of these students need. A recent EC study of future labour demand across Europe shows a consistent pattern, on the one hand of declining demand for unskilled and semi-skilled workers and, on the other hand, increased demand for technicians, third-level technical graduates and other professional workers.

There are different types of models of vocational training in European countries but they tend to have one common feature, namely a high involvement of 18-year-olds in full-time education and training. In Germany and France that figure is close to 80 per cent. In Ireland it is just under 50 per cent and in Britain just over 20 per cent.

This theme was strongly emphasised in last year's Green Paper on Education which had many excellent things to say on the importance of enterprise and technology training.

Given that Ireland featured twenty-second out of twenty-four OECD countries recently surveyed in research and development, such an emphasis is long overdue.

However, this does seem to have been downplayed in the reference to education in the Government Programme. A new Education Act has been promised, the main themes of which will be 'more democracy, devolution and openness, a genuine and meaningful role for all partners in education, including parents, and a focusing of resources towards disadvantaged areas and groups'. These are all worthy objectives. However, if we really believe that unemployment is the national priority then I would have thought the main thrust of our education policy should be to provide our youth with the life skills and technical skills which will fit them for tomorrow's world.

TAXATION POLICY has been emphasised in some of the earlier talks in this series as a serious disincentive to employment creation. To raise the issue always creates the risk of being accused of special pleading. Nevertheless, one cannot ignore the many aspects of our current taxation policy which are manifestly contrary to job-creation objectives. The Central Bank, in its submission to the Culliton Review Group, referred to the conclusion of an OECD study that none of the other twenty-four OECD countries had a tax system as biased against the use of labour as Ireland's.

Last year's finance legislation included a number of measures which might almost have been designed with the objective of discouraging long-term investment in Irish business. For example, how can it make sense to increase the capital gains tax on long-term investment profits while simultaneously reducing the capital gains tax on short-term speculative gains? Again, the proposed rescheduling of VAT payments does nothing to increase long-term revenues for the Exchequer but does create cash-flow problems felt most acutely by small businesses. Surely the objective should be to collect the necessary tax revenues by policies most consistent with the national priority of viable job creation.

MOVING ON from industrial policy there are other business-related issues that I would like to raise. I spoke earlier about some of the successes of Irish business but I would also acknowledge a serious failure in the limited trade flow that has developed with Northern Ireland. It has recently been estimated that the volume of North–South trade is approximately one-third of what it should be by analogy with similar industrial regions elsewhere. Since January 1993 this island is a single economic entity where the main trade barriers are psychological rather than physical. The potential for job creation on both sides of the border by exploiting this enlarged economic entity are real and substantial.

ANOTHER IMPORTANT factor affecting international competitiveness is our long-term exchange-rate policy. The devaluation of sterling in September 1992 brought about an extremely difficult position. Although the percentage of our trade with Britain has fallen in recent years it is still substantial. Furthermore, Britain remains our main competitor both in the home market and for exports to continental Europe.

The implications of an uncompetitive sterling relationship coupled with high interest rates are very serious for Irish business. There are also, of course, unpleasant consequences associated with alternative policies. However, we will sell our goods abroad and defend our home market only if we are competitive. If for other reasons we must live with an uncompetitive exchange rate, then we must surely address all of our costs of production if we are to maintain employment.

I MENTIONED earlier the implications for job creation of continuing productivity gains in manufacturing industry worldwide. However, we must not overlook the increasingly important contribution of the services sector. The United States has had a much better record than Europe in job creation over the past 20 years. Most of that success has been in the services sector. In Ireland, we still have a somewhat

Victorian perspective that looks upon the services sector as a parasite living off the manufacturing sector and at best providing low-level employment. Our corporate tax system reflects that bias. Leaving aside the fact that relatively low-level employment is precisely what many people need, there are many examples of high value-added service industries where Irish people are already competing internationally with considerable success, such as financial services, professional services, tourism, entertainment, health-care, third-level education, to name but a few.

ONE POINT which has struck me in looking at more successful economies overseas, such as Germany, France and Japan, is the extent of the consensus which has been developed between all of the major constituents in the economy, namely government, the civil service, business, trades unions and the banks. We have made progress recently in achieving a degree of consensus, and the NESC in particular has provided an important forum for national agreement on the need to get our public finances in order. However, many business people in Ireland still believe that their problems and concerns are rarely, if ever, fully understood by politicians and civil servants. We do still suffer from very rigid structures and a lack of mobility between the civil service and the business world. A successful industrial policy administered by Government needs to utilise fully the knowledge and experience of the business community.

This issue is particularly relevant in the context of future decisions about the allocation of EC structural funds. If this money is to have the maximum impact in improving our infrastructure (both physical and educational) we need a very strong partnership between business and Government to ensure that the funds are most effectively directed.

BEFORE CONCLUDING, there is one general point which has always mystified me. I have never heard a satisfactory explanation as to how it can be sensible to suffer an unemployment rate of 20 per cent and at the same time to tolerate

a wide range of social problems and inadequate infrastructure. One of the top legislative priorities of the new
United States Administration defined by President Clinton is
the introduction of a form of voluntary national service. This
is seen as a way of improving the quality of the future workforce, thus improving United States competitiveness, and
equally as a way of fighting urban decay and tackling huge
social problems such as slum-rebuilding, refuse clearance,
feeding and housing the homeless, caring for the elderly and
providing assistance to nurses, police officers and social
workers. Clearly it has cost implications but the alternative
of paying people to do nothing, while ignoring many of the
tasks that could be tackled by paying them a little more, has
to be fundamentally flawed.

AT A more general level, there is perhaps an even more
important lesson to be drawn from the new administration
in the United States, namely its emphasis on national economic policy. The new President is committed to giving economic policy the same priority and attention as national security had in the years of the Cold War.

If the new United States Administration, in charge of the
most productive economy in the world, with an unemployment rate less than half that in Ireland, has decided to give
this priority to economic policy, how much more important
should it be for us in Ireland? Surely it should mean that
national policies in so many areas, whether education, taxation, exchange rates, social welfare, labour legislation or
others, should all be critically examined to ensure that they
are focused on the objective of creating long-term viable jobs
in Ireland by facilitating and supporting an effective business response.

If we were really concerned about the gravity of the unemployment crisis and the threat it poses to our society, this
is the approach we would adopt. The question is, do we
really have that concern?

Footnotes

[1] *Work is the Key: Towards an Economy That Needs Everyone,* The Irish Episcopal Conference, Veritas Publications, Dublin, 1992.

12. The Future of Work

Paddy Walley

MANY OF OUR traditional images, theories and structures in relation to the world of work and the economy are in urgent need of re-evaluation. This is due to a variety of factors, including the success of industrialisation in vastly uplifting the productivity, output and levels of affluence of modern economies, the changes in patterns of global investment, the changing role of women, the emergence of new technologies and the growing environmental awareness. In the process of re-evaluation it will be helpful to be aware that most of our present thinking on the role, nature and structure of work was formed to explain and energise the industrial revolution. Due to the nature of the human perceptual process, we tend to view our inherited ways of thinking about society and organising society as almost biological principles and eternal truths. However, things have changed since the industrial revolution began, and right now, society is again changing fast. If we want to capitalise on the employment opportunities these changes offer, we must find new ways of thinking. It is my hope throughout this lecture to help open new ways of looking at the world of work.

I will first look at some implications of the affluence of modern society for the world of work. The process of industrialisation has resulted in a standard of living in industrialised countries for the majority of people which was undreamt of in the past: this can be seen in the levels of material consumption, in access to housing, health-care, education, in terms of the increased longevity of life and the amount of discretionary leisure time available to people. The length of the working week and working year has declined significantly: in Germany the working year is just 1500 hours, in the USA it is 1800 hours, and in both countries the figure is still declining. This compares with a working year of 3000 hours at the turn of the century. The amount of discretionary time in the life of the average worker has increased by 70 per cent since the turn of the century. The length of life has increased by ten years in the past four decades. The result of this increased longevity, combined with the contraction in the length of time spent in jobs, has greatly increased the amount of discretionary time in people's lives. The activities undertaken in this discretionary time have a very significant effect on the products produced and the nature of employment created. Leisure activities have become a significant source of demand for new products. And the growing number of old people will also change the pattern of demand, of products manufactured and of sources of employment.

There is a growing concern in relation to the quality of performance, design, service, image and the uniqueness of products. People in affluent societies want more individualised products. This has changed the definition of the competitiveness of products and services from being uni-dimensional, based on price, to one which sees price as only one of the factors determining competitiveness. It has also changed the process of production and the kinds of employment production provides. For example, research, design, marketing and customer service have become increasingly important aspects of product development. An OECD study estimates that up to 80 per cent of value added in manufacturing is in the service end; most of the employment generated is also in the services, not in the direct process of manufacturing itself.

The new affluence has also created demand for services in financial management, in cultural products and activities, in education, tourism and health-care. Employment in affluent societies is primarily in services either to production or to people. In the EC, in the period 1985–90, industry's share of employment dropped from 40 per cent to 31 per cent and services' share rose from 43 per cent to 61 per cent. In the USA, by 1988, services' share of employment had reached 70 per cent, while industry's share was 27 per cent and agriculture was only 3 per cent. Within the EC, the proportion employed in services was considerably higher in more prosperous countries than in poorer countries: the figures are 65–70 per cent in Denmark and the Netherlands, but less than 55 per cent in Spain and Ireland. The implications for the future trend of employment and shape of employment in Ireland are clearly immense.

The changes in the structure and balance of employment have been caused not just by the affluence of society; new technologies have had their impact as well. I will now look at some of the developments which new technologies are bringing. In simple terms, the development and application of new technologies are creating new jobs, new products, new ways of organising work and production, a global economy and new ways of generating employment. New technologies are also resulting in the disappearance of many traditional skills and industries. They have changed the basis of competitiveness. They are replacing the relatively stable, centralised and slowly changing industrial society with an economy in which change is more frequent and constant, and structures which are more decentralised.

The application of new technologies eliminates the least complex, repetitive and labour-intensive jobs; this has resulted in the virtual disappearance of blue-collar, labour-intensive manufacturing systems; brawn is being replaced by brains as the source of value in production. Information technology eliminates the necessity for many of the activities concerned with information dissemination and control which provides layers of management and supervisory jobs. The result is the disappearance of much of middle management and supervisory jobs; organisations become flatter with fewer layers between shop floor and senior management. The hierarchical 'military' model of organisation is being replaced by the 'symphony orchestra' model in which the conductor's role is to harmonise and evoke the creativity of the members. Similarly, the role of management is to facilitate the innovative capacity of the workforce and the development of their skills. The workforce is being seen as the resource of the organisation, not as a cost as in classical economics, but as the central wealth, the source of value.

Information technology makes possible the emergence of a new system of production to replace the production system of Henry Ford; a system of production which aims to be highly responsive to people's needs and highly flexible as well. The short-run manufacturing of a number of products is replacing the continuous production of unchanging products as in mass production. Production is aimed at niche short-life markets. Speed of response to rapidly changing needs and uniqueness of products are important aspects of competitiveness in the affluent society. New technologies also facilitate the integration of a much broader range of activities within the manufacturing process. Design, marketing, customer service, in addition to direct process activities, are now included in the definition of production. New technologies have increased the knowledge content of products and reduced the labour and raw materials content. The result is that the creation, organisation and dissemination of knowledge is the primary source of employment. The employment available in the future will require a higher level of skills than in the past.

Since products and methods of production will change rapidly and continuously in this highly technical society, several career changes will be a common fact of the employment experience. Retraining and upgrading of skills will be an imperative for everyone in a society where innovation is a primary dynamic. Education and learning will play a central role in the life of individuals and society. The capacity to learn will be a critical skill for individuals and organisations. Learning will become a growing part of our concept of work as more of working time will be devoted to learning. The increased focus in the workplace on learning and the growth of non-work time in people's lives will mean that learning will become the central business of society. Learning will be the new form of labour; the learning organisation is the organisation of the future.

An important new learning challenge, both collectively and individually, will be how to manage personal and group transitions in a creative and humane way. The world of work now emerging with new technologies, products and processes will bring continuous change in the jobs available. The decline of the old production systems, which became very pervasive since the 1970s, resulted in severe dislocation and suffering for many individuals and groups throughout Europe. The closure of industries meant loss of income and sense-of-self as people's jobs and skills disappeared. For many it was the closing of a way of life, a whole culture; whole communities became deskilled and unemployed. The framing of the closures in the language of recession rather than of the change in the economic process added to their sense of failure. In many areas throughout Europe the realisation that central government structures were unable to cope positively with this process of change had the positive effect of sparking the emergence of local development organisations in communities, cities and regions. The result has been that the local area has become an important part of the employment creation scene, and new networks of alliances have formed locally and across Europe to generate employment. This process of restructuring and relearning will now be a continuous part of the developed world's economies as new products and technologies emerge and old ones disappear.

An efficient and humane employment policy will create structures at central and local levels to predict and manage the process of change. Innovation on new sources of employment should now be an active part of the management of companies and organisations and part of the awareness of everyone in work. Invention of employment should become part of everyone's activities. The effective, preventative management of the changes brought about by changing markets and new technology should become the central part of a policy on unemployment as it is very difficult to integrate people once they become unemployed for any length of time. It is worth remembering that only 30 per cent of new employment created in Europe since 1985 has gone to unemployed people; 70 per cent went to new entrants to the labour force. The percentage of long-term unemployed has grown and the tendency is for those to be located in particular communities which makes re-integration even more difficult. Employers are reluctant to employ people who have been out of work for long spells. Therefore, an employment policy, in addition to designing future employment, should ensure that no one has to be outside employment for long. It should actively manage transitions with the close involvement of the social partners. It is interesting to note that Denmark has developed a system which guarantees access to retraining and work opportunities within a maximum of 6 months of redundancy. The most desirable strategy is to have the retraining take place while people are still employed.

The next area I would like to look at is the changing pattern of global investment. The changes which have occurred in the global investment patterns since the 1970s have changed Ireland's definition of the world of work quite substantially. Since the 1960s a central aspect of Ireland's policy of employment creation was to provide an environment which would attract multinationals requiring large inputs of unskilled labour. The combination of low wages and significant levels of grant aid was seen as the decisive factor in our competitive advantage to attract this employment. The opening, since the 1970s, of the countries of Asia, Africa and Eastern Europe to foreign investment, and their integration into the global economy, altered the definition of low-cost labour. Ireland became a high-wage society relative to these countries as wages there are only a fraction of wages in Ireland. Industries requiring large quantities of low-skilled labour moved there. To compete with these countries for this form of employment we would need to lower wages to levels of around £500 per year. This would involve us leaving the EC and rolling back decades of social progress. This is not realistic. When we talk about 'jobs', it is not jobs at any price, presumably. There would be no shortage of jobs if we were not concerned about the quality of the work or the level of the remuneration. The number of jobs is not a measure of the wealth of a country; it is the type of jobs, not just the ability to employ citizens at low wages that is decissive for economic prosperity.

In recognition of this changed investment reality, we need a new strategy for employment creation which is not focused on Ireland as a passive, low-wage society, depending on large employers from outside who will require large numbers of people. We need a new vision of Ireland in relation to employment, a vision which can release the creativity and enterprise of people and generate an environment which is proactive in relation to employment creation. It is a vision of Ireland with a high level of education, skills and innovative motivation and capacity. It is a workforce with high skills, determining our competitive advantage and generating and attracting appropriate employment. A high-wage policy gives a competitive advantage in this knowledge society. It will attract these people who will in turn generate the new industries of the future.

Our present strategies are still primarily focused on multinationals. The result of the change in global investment patterns is that many of the multinationals we now attract are highly capital-intensive with little labour content. The statistics of their investment and their exports certainly improve our economic growth figures: for example, we have had the highest economic growth in the EC and the OECD for a number of years. However, there has been no increase in the employment that economists projected would follow economic growth. There obviously is a need for a much closer examination of the employment accompanying this type of investment. At the end of the day, the £600 million we spend a year on our industrial policy may in fact be impoverishing our culture through the grant aids paid out to these companies. For the future, proclamations that the shortage of employment is being caused by a shortage of economic growth, or that more growth will effectively mean more employment, are obviously not true. The *type* of economic activity is a critical issue as to whether or not economic growth generates employment. This is a fact that we cannot afford to forget.

The fourth area I wish to examine in this lecture is the changing role of men and women. There is a growing demand from women for paid employment. This is coming from a variety of sources. For a start, women's view of their role in society is changing. Increasing numbers are no longer satisfied to be the unpaid carers in the home, dependent on the male as the source of income for the family. They want the experience of the social relations, the status of paid work and the sense of independence deriving from having their own income. The growth in male unemployment is also bringing pressures on women to support the family. The increase in divorce and the number of single parent families is also bringing pressures for women to earn income, as most single parents are women.

Let me give you some figures. In Denmark, the UK and Germany, one household in ten with a child under the age of 10 is a one-parent family. In the period 1960–86, divorce rates doubled in Denmark and Germany, trebled in Belgium and France, and increased sixfold and ninefold in the UK and Portugal respectively. There are 21 million women in the active 25–49 age group in the EC who are not registered as unemployed, but a growing number of whom are seeking paid employment. This will be a growing social and political issue.

The issue of equal access to paid employment by women is part of the wider debate on the value of work, on parenting in the home and on the changing role of men and women. Increasingly, men wish to take a more active role in parenting and to spend more time with their children or elderly parents. They feel that men lost out in their relationships with their children due to the rigid work structures of industrial society. The changes needed in relation to work to

enable a greater sharing of work responsibilities between
men and women will involve restructuring the social infrastructure of child-care facilities, education and training opportunities, social security, school hours, attitudes of employers and changes in other areas of society. Caring for the
growing number of elderly people is also becoming a significant issue in Europe as the number of elderly people
grows. The lifespan in Europe has increased by 10 years in
the past 40 years. This factor will have to be considered as
well.

Throughout the 1980s, women's share in employment
grew in every country in the EC. Women now account for 38
per cent of paid employment in the EC, and this is growing
rapidly. Of the 10 million new jobs created in the period
1985–9, 30 per cent went to men, 70 per cent to women. In
the period 1965–90 the number of women in paid employment grew from 39 million to 52 million, while the number
of men actually decreased from 83 million to 82 million. Despite these advances, the participation rate of women in paid
employment in the EC is still only 45 per cent, compared to
75 per cent for men.

Women are also still restricted to a narrow range of employment opportunities. Much of the growth of women's
participation in paid employment was due to the growth of
part-time work in the services sector. For some women this
is very desirable as it enables them to combine child-
minding with paid employment. For others this is not a
choice as there are no full-time jobs available. Furthermore,
the gap between the wages paid to men and women is still
substantial in most countries in the EC. And a final factor is
that a much larger percentage of women's work is part-time,
although the percentage varies widely throughout the Community. For example, it accounts for 8–12 per cent of female
employment in Italy and Spain; 40 per cent in Denmark and
the UK and over 60 per cent in the Netherlands.

The workplace today has become much more feminine,
a trend which is helped by the fact that most new work requires mental rather than physical input and by the growth

in part-time contracts. The areas of work which are being wiped out by new technologies and work practices are in the areas which were traditionally occupied by males, namely the blue-collar workers and middle-management. It is worth noting that up to the mid-1800s the idea of the male being the sole provider of income for the household did not exist: women were the main earners through part-time work in the markets. Things are coming full circle.

A final force which will significantly affect the world of work is the growing environmental awareness. The evidence of global warming, ozone depletion, destruction of rivers and forests caused by industrial production are all resulting in environmental controls of production by governments and increasing discrimination by people in relation to the environmental effects of the products they buy. While in traditional economic thinking unlimited growth was both socially desirable and acceptable, this idea is being replaced by the idea of sustainable growth. This will involve creative accounting systems which give a more complete measure of the cost of economic progress to the environment than traditional measures which saw increased output as being indicative of social progress whatever the environmental effects. It will also involve legislation in relation to production which will ensure that patterns of production do not destroy natural resources or cause harmful pollution.

An interesting innovation in this respect was undertaken in California, whereby companies are given positive environmental credits which become part of the companies' assets. These credits are lost if any environmental pollution or damage is caused and they are advertised as part of the stock value of the company. The building of environmental awareness into the shaping of the economy will affect the composition and location of economic activity, the structure of employment and the nature of jobs. It will affect research undertaken, technologies developed, products produced and the type of agriculture practised.

The developed economies are already moving in the direction of economic activities and technologies which are environmentally more friendly than industrial systems. The use of new materials in production has declined dramatically. Japan increased its industrial production by two-and-a-half times between 1965 and 1985, but did not increase its use of raw materials and energy. In 1920 raw materials and energy made up 60 per cent of the central product of that time, the car. The raw material and energy content of the central product of the present, the microchip, is 2 per cent. Indeed many new products use little energy or raw materials at all: they are just information or services. The new biotechnology uses no energy at all. So production and consumption are shifting from being energy- and raw-materials-intensive to being knowledge-intensive.

The implications of active environmental management for employment will be significant. Being ecologically friendly can give companies and countries competitive advantages, for example the ecologically friendly aspect of motor car advertising. In addition, environmental management will directly provide new employment. It is estimated that 15 million people are employed directly in environmental protection and represent about 1 per cent of both employment and GNP in the EC, with twice that many in environmental related employment. It is projected that a major growth in jobs in this area of 1 per cent a year will occur in water management and water treatment. That alone is significant.

As more awareness of the environment is growing, new areas of activity are emerging. There is the restoration of historical buildings, reviving natural systems, creating nature reserves, developing sophisticated technological-based systems of pollution control and designing environmental impact studies for planning and leisure activities. The evidence is that the incorporation of measures to protect the environment into the economic activities of a region or country enhances its competitiveness for new industry and jobs. The very process of doing so equips society with new skills and networks to manage more complex and innovative systems. In some ways it creates a new intellectual and a new technological capacity resulting in new enterprise. An example of this can be found in the Ruhr area of Germany which cleaned up industrial pollution and created 100,000 jobs. An environmentally sophisticated development policy attracts industries of the future. These in turn bring high quality jobs.

At the outset of this paper I mentioned the urgent need for a re-evaluation of our traditional images, assumptions and ways of thinking about the world of work. I have focused on five areas to give an awareness of the possibilities for innovation. These possibilities will only be realised if we open our thinking to the new information I have described in this lecture. If we do not open our way of looking at the future, then we will inevitably reproduce the past with all its problems, not least the problem of unemployment. It will require a new thought process if we are to take on the employment challenge of the years ahead. I would like to end with a point made by Jacques Delors in his recent book, *Our Europe*.[1] He pointed out that 3 out of every 4 products and services which will be consumed in the year 2000 do not yet exist. This essentially means that the future world of work will not be inherited but is being invented right now. The possibilities for employment will be limited only by our own limitations of imagination and commitment.

Footnotes
[1] Jacques Delors, *Our Europe*, Verso, London and New York, 1992.

13. The Larger World Economy

John Kenneth Galbraith

THERE COMES A TIME when one should step back and seek to envisage the larger world scene. In concentrating on detail, we, on occasion, lose sight of the larger picture. When, as now, we live in a time of marked economic change, even of recent revolution, this larger view is especially to be sought. That is my effort in this lecture, which I am honoured to give today.

As was Gaul, the modern economic world is divided into three parts. There are, first, the poor lands of the planet – those variously characterised as the undeveloped countries, more optimistically as the developing countries and, with intense economic neutrality, as the South.

There are, next, the relatively advanced countries that are now emerging to a market system from comprehensive socialism, commonly called Communism. These are the countries of Eastern Europe that were once behind the now-vanished Iron Curtain, and the republics of the former Soviet Union.

Finally, there are the fortunate lands, those that have escaped from the poverty and stagnation that, without much change, afflicted all the people of the world until a couple of centuries ago. They include Western Europe, the United States and the English-speaking countries in general, and Japan, Taiwan and the other developing lands of the Pacific Basin. It is the world to which Ireland belongs, as I am privileged to say today.

In looking at the larger world and its present problems, I seek to do so without the constraints of ideology. This is not the age of great theoretical systems. Those who so believe are in escape from thought – and all past experience. This, pre-eminently, is the age of intelligent pragmatism. The economic problem must be examined and judged not for its conformance to theoretical pattern but for its efficacy in the particular time and context. I urge against the frequent retreat from thought to a presumed controlling doctrine.

THE POOR lands – those of the South – are the most difficult case. Suddenly released from colonial authority, they were left with the most demanding task of our time. That was putting in place efficient, effective, non-corrupt and stable democratic government, this being the essential basis of economic development and human contentment. Nothing so destroys all hope for economic wellbeing as corrupt and/ or totalitarian governments that are concerned, inevitably, not with economic and social progress but with consolidating and holding their own authority. This, one notes, can be the burden of governments ostensibly of the left and of the right. And nothing so destroys both people and progress as internal conflict.

One cites here the sad experience of much of Africa and of other ex-colonial lands. There was a major mistake in the process of decolonisation: time and effort should have been committed, perhaps under the auspices of the United Nations, to helping guide former colonial governments to a stable democratic alternative. Only those countries that have had a stable democratic alternative to colonial rule – Singapore, Costa Rica, India, a few others – have had a reliable rate of economic development and an otherwise tolerable existence.

There was another error. Far too much emphasis was placed on industrial investment and development, far too little on education and human investment. Once it was understood: an educated populace is the first requirement for economic progress. That essential fact was forgotten;

impressive steel mills, large hydroelectric dams, glistening airports, were too often sited amid ignorant people. I have previously made the point: in this world there is no literate population that is poor, no illiterate population that is other than poor.

Finally, in many cases there was too much attention to urban development and wellbeing at the expense of agriculture. In some instances, prices were kept low to serve the presumed interest of an urban proletariat. This, too, was a prime error ending in food insufficiency and hunger. Of all economic needs, that for food is the first.

If we are to talk effectively about economic development now and in the years to come, the emphasis must be on political stability, on human investment and on sound, sensible agricultural policy. These, we now know, are the prime requirements of progress.

In the worst cases of internal disorder and cruelty, we must have a new and internationally sanctioned suspension of sovereignty. Where, as recently for long years in Lebanon, Mozambique and Ethiopia, now disastrously in Somalia and Bosnia, there has been human cruelty and slaughter, there must be effective action to arrest it. There must be a United Nations mandate for governing countries that do not and cannot govern themselves. International law outlaws attack by one country on another; such attack is not within the accepted rights of sovereign power. No longer can domestic conflict and the associated starvation and death be protected by sovereign authority. Sovereignty must be suspended until peace is restored. This involves no slight change in public attitudes. The change is now overdue.

TURNING TO Eastern Europe and the republics of the former Soviet Union, one sees here an intensely difficult and, in some respects, the most dangerous transition in economic history – the movement from comprehensive socialism to the market economy. It will also stand as one of the most misguided of social actions. It has, for the moment, come close to the exchange of a poorly working economic system for none at all.

In the early days of this change, some – I was one – pleaded for gradualism, for a considered release of economic life to the market. First should have come services, less urgent consumer goods, and, as possible, agriculture. Then, larger industry, when effective alternatives to the price-controlled and command economy had been brought into being, including the requisite financial and marketing structures.

Instead there has been a sudden plunge toward what was thought the capitalist miracle. It has turned out to be no miracle; rather, there has come a period of grave economic deprivation and hardship. Those who urged this course of action, including the International Monetary Fund and not a few ideologically motivated scholars from the United States, could not have had a better design for giving capitalism and democracy a bad name. And from the United States, as also from Japan and other countries, adequate economic help was not forthcoming, help that might have eased the transition. Future generations will marvel at how financial assistance that might have saved democracy and the market system was kept committed instead to no-longer-needed military expenditure. No one should have doubt as to the danger. It is that, capitalism and democracy having been seen as synonymous with grave hardship, there will be escape into some new form of totalitarian rule.

I would urge help to the former Soviet republics as well as to the Eastern European countries. And I would urge that this not be conditional on specified market reforms. Here, above all, is the case for pragmatic accommodation to circumstance.

I TURN now to the fortunate countries of the world, including the one to which I speak. We, too, have economic problems; they are central to any consistent and compelling discussion. Let us also have them in perspective; they are small as compared with those I have just adumbrated. Two – one relatively unimportant, one urgent – now capture our attention.

The smaller problem, seemingly vital in Europe but of worldwide concern, involves capital movements, currency relationships and the marked instability in the foreign exchanges. This, I think, will be recalled one day as a minor blip in the larger economic history of our time.

The controlling circumstance is that monetary goals – stable exchange rates – can be achieved only after there is an alignment of internal social and economic policies, including, in particular, fiscal, budget and employment policies. As long as these are individually variant – and, as now, often radically so – stable exchange rates are quite impossible. In Europe a common unit of exchange is superficially a very attractive idea; that it can come before an alignment of the controlling internal policies will stand as one of the major economic miscalculations of the age.

The broad thrust toward closer economic relations and to economic unification, notably in Europe, will continue; modern capitalism with its massive trade and travel, its extensive capital movements, its close communications and its transnational corporate enterprises is, by its nature (and unlike onetime feudal and peasant agriculture or early industrialism), an international system. From it comes the basic thrust to a civilised internationalism – this despite the fact that regressive nationalism still accords a greatly welcomed voice to the politically articulate but mentally bereft. As this great economic thrust proceeds, there could one day be the unity in domestic policies that will allow of stability in exchanges and in Europe a common medium of exchange. The results of the premature effort, the consequences of which have been so recently evident, will stand as the minor historical blip I have already mentioned.

THE FAR more serious matter is the current depression in economic activity. This has persisted in the United States for two long years and more. And while we must accept our role as to the origin, depression is now a painful fact in the other English-speaking countries, in Ireland, and it is a threat to the industrially developed world at large. We must, as an exercise in common everyday caution and good sense, accept in the larger world the proposition that Keynes articulated: the modern economy does not necessarily find its equilibrium at full employment; it is perfectly possible for it to enter upon and stabilise itself at an underemployment equilibrium. After two long years this possibility must be recognised. Some modest recent improvement in economic activity in the United States should not be taken to deny the possibility.

There must also be reflection on the causes of this continuing depression. They, notably in the United States, include the speculative splurge of the 1980s – the mergers and acquisitions and leveraged-buyout mania that left corporations with the heavy burden of debt under which they now struggle and which they service at the expense of new investment. There was also the real property boom and collapse, with its counterpart in other countries, including Canada, Britain and notably Japan. From the above, especially in the United States, came weakness in the banking system that negated central-bank efforts to expand bank borrowing and associated economic activity. We are now seeing, as often before, that monetary policy, while it can have an effect on inflation, is nearly useless against deflation and depression. One cites again the relevant metaphor: there is a great difference between pulling on a string and shoving on a string.

Finally, in the Reagan years there was a major transfer of income from the poor to the rich. The upper 1 per cent of American families captured 70 per cent of the growth in average family income in the years 1977–88. The share going to the poor declined. Income going to the rich is not reliably spent; it may be saved, and savings, given the caution of the time, are not reliably invested. A reasonably equitable distribution of income is socially just and a contribution to political tranquillity. It is also economically functional.

AS I speak, a new administration has just come to power in the United States. It has only one major choice as to policy. That is either to allow the underemployment equilibrium to stand, with the barren hope that time will somehow work a cure, or to move aggressively to reduce unemployment and renew economic growth. For the latter result there is only one sure course of action. That is to set aside for the time concern as to the deficit in the federal budget and, by government action and expenditure, put people to work.

In the United States, our roads, bridges, schools, railroads, urban transport, airports and housing stock, particularly the latter, are all in poor and sometimes even dangerous condition. And our states and cities are spreading fear and hardship by curtailing essential services, including, notably, education and welfare support to the poor. The only way to break the depressive equilibrium that does not depend on theoretical formulation is to move strongly on these needs.

This, in the short run, will increase the public deficit and the public debt, attitudes on both of which have now reached paranoiac proportions. These attitudes must, for the time, be ignored.

When prosperity returns, the deficit should be reduced. Among the errors of the past years was the running of a large such deficit when its supporting effect on the economy was not needed. All countries must have a disciplined will to adjust taxation and expenditure to the prevailing economic condition. For now, to repeat, the deficit must be accepted. The economic activity and employment so provided is the only design for dealing with the depressive equilibrium that, as I have said, does not depend on fragile theory. It goes directly to the needed result. I venture to think that this policy and this discipline have a wider relevance and application, not excluding in the country to which I speak today.

In the United States some gain in employment can be had from a shift of expenditure from military to civilian employment. Expenditure on exotic weaponry, now devoid of any justification, is a very inefficient way of creating employment. I would also urge, as did Governor Clinton as a candidate, an increase of taxes on the rich. This does not seriously reduce aggregate demand and has a benign social aspect. Taxation is in accordance with ability to pay. Maybe – a fugitive thought – the resulting effort to maintain after-tax income by the very affluent could have an affirmative incentive effect. Certainly this is as probable as the erstwhile supply-side argument that the rich needed the incentive ef fect of more income.

In the longer run, this course of action will increase public wealth – there are both the things built and the expansive effect on economic output in general. The Japanese have recently announced such a programme. In Canada a conservative government has let it be known that it is thinking along these lines. I raise the point as to Ireland. But, in any case, I come back to my main thesis: there is nothing else of equally certain effect.

IN THE great sweep of modern capitalism, there is a further change which we experience, which is inevitable and which some despair. That is the movement of older, established, labour-intensive industry from the old countries to the new. The history of the last 150 years and more has been of the movement of such industry, old and new, from Britain to the Continent, on to the United States, then to Japan, then to other countries of the Pacific Basin and notably to Korea and Taiwan. The movement now continues to Thailand, Malaysia and, with potentially perhaps the greatest consequence, to India.

The basis of this movement is clear: mass industry is constantly in pursuit of a fresh and eager labour force, one that is eagerly in escape from the true oppressions of primitive peasant agriculture and from older, bureaucratic management to the leaner, fresher, often more innovative managements of the new countries.

This movement is a fixed source of concern and even despair in the older countries. There can be no question that for some in those countries it is a cause of dislocation and hardship. It must be recognised, however, as one of the great and inescapable features of modern industrial capitalism. It does not leave the older countries, such as Ireland, devoid. The higher ranges of technology, of design, of entertainment and of education remain with them. It is important, however, that this great process be understood and not be the occasion for ill-considered preventives as protective action. Let us see that there is a broad international division of labour in the modern economic world.

As to Ireland, among the modern nation states I would note that it still offers an eager, well-educated labour force. That, I trust, in contrast with some of the other advanced countries, will be a continuing source of strength. And there are further steps. Beyond mass-production industry lies the world of good design, something that was very important in the post-war success, for example, of Italy and which I would again urge for the country to which I here speak. And there is the world of entertainment, including that of visitors from abroad. And of advanced technology which should be supported as may be necessary by the state. These are the next great steps along the path of economic progress. To these I command the closest attention, not only in my own country but here in Ireland as well.